The Poet Inside Me

The Poet Inside Me

Simran Kalita

The Poet Inside Me

First Edition

Copyright © 2025 Simran Kalita

Cover art by Antara Baruah

ISBN 979-8-218-61047-0

Printed in the United States of America

For ordering information, bulk purchases, and speaking engagements, contact the author at:
simran.r.kalita@gmail.com
simrankalita.com
@simranrakhee

First Printing, 2025

Simran Kalita

To my younger self—the most important love in my life—
and my Koka (Grandfather in Assamese), the first writer in
my family. This is an ode to the magic I've carried in my
pocket since I was a little girl.

Thank you, Fiona, Ritu, and Elena, for being my second set of eyes in this process. Thank you, Ashley, for inspiring me to do this. Thank you, Antara Ba, for your beautiful art.

Lastly, to my precious students, whom I spent everyday looking after while crafting this book—I love you, Aleenah, Momo, Hailey, Kiki, Telilah, Raylea, Abby, Apollo, Nevada, Trinity, Khabir, Olivia, Mila, Theo, Luana, Jackson, Lucas, Joey, Hayes, Willy, Graham, Olive, and Zaleiah.

Table of Contents

Love in every word

Simran Kalita

I never told you

I'm writing this because
It's been so much time
And in this solitary
I've come to realize you never even got to know
How much I wanted you

I did so much to prove to you
The woman I could be
When I never got to show you
The woman I am
Or the feelings hidden underneath

So now I get to say
Everything that's been captured in my brain
With no one left to listen
I hope you can give me just this second
To read the things that made you iridescent to me:

You have what looks like a storm cloud that envelopes your
body
Though people may think it is your guardedness
It is simply all the thoughts and burdens that you carry
And while you mistake it for your own weakness
I can see how it is your armor, strong and made of titanium

You once told me I have an aura of comfort
Well, your aura is one of strength and solitude
Wrapped with charisma and kindness
People do not realize the pure, loving heart that you possess
To forgive those unworthy and those that brought regret

And while you know the powers of your smile
Let me indulge a little
Your smile could make my heart skip a beat
And when you look at me with your wondering eyes
I forget everything I am about to say

You make me nervous in a way I have no control over
Tall and mighty have not made me flinch
But something about your being
Takes me to a place where I can only fantasize you and I
Can't you tell I hate this feeling

The feeling that you have all the power
And even though you don't, you still do
Your chiseled jaw and alluring frame
Your big, pointed nose
Your lips that give my own competition

Your eyes
God I could write poems & novels & movie scripts about
those eyes
I could go on and on
Don't let me, for they are not mine to peer into
The way they capture me with every glance

Those dark eyes
With so much soul in them, so many things to say
Though you only get out a word or two
Billions of emotions plague your mind
Why don't you let them subside

You have a piercing gaze
That awakens every sensation in my body
I want to run to you
But I also want to run from you
You're too powerful

I'm always nervous to be around you
When you smile at me
Or tell me something that makes me feel noble
I don't find myself more beautiful than in that moment
No one lifts me the way that you do

When I'm with you, I feel powerful too
I feel like all the words that you say are true
And maybe I am as amazing as you think me to be
Maybe I do possess the qualities that you so carelessly
called me
By the way, you've got me thinking and rethinking every
thought

I love seeing you happy
I know I called your laugh goofy, but can you tell that I
love the way it sounds
I was only being mean to get your attention
I hide it well, don't I
But you're the only one whose simple presence can make
my heart fly

I will always support you, my strength is not wavering
Though I may not always be there
That is my choice, so I can be there for myself as well
Because if I were to love you wholeheartedly
There is a risk that I would forget myself in that infatuation

You mean more to me than almost everyone else in this
world
And that is what scares me
Because not only do I know you have not asked for this
I also know that if you asked, I would give up everything
And I know that's probably silly

I've always been so afraid
To let you know, to let you know how I feel
Maybe I should've let it go
Instead of letting all of it build up
Don't tell me that this means I'm in love

I don't even know what it means to be in love
When no one has dared to take me on
Nor have I dared to let my passions ignite
Don't let what others have scoffed at
Be rephrased as love in your eyes

Don't you know that I am fine all alone
And it's only when I am with you
Or when I am thinking about you
Or when I am dreaming about you
Or when I am fantasizing us

When I am telling you about the things that I do
Experiencing memories with you
Reliving old ones in my head
Wishing you were here instead of in my head
That one can see I am fully captured by you

Please forgive me
If I have crossed a line too many times
It's just that you make me feel a certain way
As though I am carved of gold
And you are the sculptor

I keep misreading the expression in your eyes
I let myself believe that the joy when you see me
Is proof that you desperately need me
That the admiration when your eyes—my favorite thief—
take me in
Is the love you so carefully draw me with

Simran Kalita

No one can love you the way that I do
That is my promise
Though my hand is not in yours
It lies right behind you
Always there to catch you in case you fall

And leaving you alone
Does not mean that I have left you
It just means you do not want me here anymore
And so I must go
To keep myself from becoming a martyr

You are made of gold to me
A type of gold that will never rust
The dark shade that covers your layers
How I wish I could feel your skin with my own hands
You remind me of a dream I once had

It sounds corny but no one else understands
No one gets why I feel this way about you
Or why you don't feel the same way
Or why I still seem to stay
But I was never one to listen to others

No matter how much they would stop me
I have a mind of my own
And my mind only listens to this heart
This heart said it belongs to you
Now what am I to do

No one sees you the way that I do
I believe that you have the power to lead a fort
I've told you this before
Don't know why I think this of you
Have no idea what the reasoning even is

I just know that there must be some meaning behind all this
Because, truly, if it were not for you
I never would've had anything I do today
My songs are lyrics about you
The reason I ever wrote a song was because of you

The poems I've written the past few years
All you
And it's not to say that I've been pining for you all this
time
But you're the first person to inspire me to do something
beautiful with my life
I already had a plan, but you made me want to start living it

All the other things I wanted
Felt like a faraway dream
But seeing your face light up when I told you about it
Made me want to keep going, made me feel like you were
part of the plan
And now I feel I owe you my identity

I guess this is just what happens
When you meet people in life
I'm sure that you've felt this way before me
But please don't fault me
I didn't ask to choose you first

Sometimes feelings just override us
When they take control, they hit you with a full force
And sometimes I just feel robbed
Taken from my protected enclosure, my heart was now
yours
Now, the only one who has a right to me is you

I can't shake this feeling
And I tried so hard, I really did
I tried keeping it from you
I tried giving it to someone else
Hell, I even tried to make it numb

Unfortunately, that's a problem for another day
Now, I'm just here to tell you about my day
My days, where I do miss you
But I'm doing so well
I'm doing everything I promised myself

I wish you were closer so I could tell you
I know you want to know
But I'm afraid that getting too close will make it hard to let
go
I'm meeting new people, leading new lives
Lots of plans and even unopposed to meeting a new man

It's not that I compare anyone against you
But I'm waiting until I find someone who makes me feel
Like fire when I walk into a room
I don't know why I always felt that with you
I'm waiting until someone loves me back equally in every
possible manner

It doesn't mean anything to try to get back at you
Why would you even care
I used to want to do that to you, but then I realized that's
stupid
We're too old to play these games
I'm too headstrong to pause my life to make you jealous,
even though I could

The Poet Inside Me

I know you know me so well
But not well enough
You couldn't tell I was falling for you
And you couldn't tell that I was slowly disappearing
I can't tell if you made me lose myself or find it

Now I am at a crossroads
And every road with you in it seems like a
Safe bet, not that we're together in any capacity
But every road without you
Is just too scary to choose

I'll keep my distance
I swear I will
But you better not tell me things to make me think you care
You know that painting that you promised you'd buy one day
Even that, you have a right to

A lot of those poems are about you
Now don't go thinking you're the only one
But you can bask in the pride for a bit
Truly, some of my most breathtaking poems are about you
I'll have you know I'm not as crazy as those poems, though

A lot of it is imagination
Or using one memory to create a story
A lot of the feelings aren't even feelings I've experienced
I just love to embellish
But nothing about how I feel for you is fake

Nothing I have ever said
Nor that I have ever done
Or I have ever hoped for
Has ever been untrue
Just so you know how I feel for you

Simran Kalita

I hope we remain friends for a long time
And I'm sure I will meet my soulmate one day
I guess the last thing I never told you
Is how grateful I am for bumping into you
Thank you for, at one point, being the one.

Love Language

To sleep so close to you
without touching you

To walk so close to you
to only feel your shadow

To not say a word to you
but laugh at all your jokes

To watch you silently
Your eyes, your smile, your every move
but never be near you

That is my love language.

quietly, he captured me

Alphabet

Every letter of your name has a new meaning
Every curve has its own charms
From the way you reach up high
To the line that makes a slope
From the repetition you contain
To the downturn that it creates
I know this much because it's the only word I can
remember
And languages come easily to me
But your name remains the same no matter the country
I love your name in every dialect I know
Play around with the pronunciations and the throw
But each time it comes out closest to the sweetest note
And I'm also a singer so I should know
The letters in many words I may forget
But the way your name makes me feel
Feels more like I should keep it a secret
Is it a code or a magic phrase to unlock some treasure
I use it as my password because it's the easiest thing to
remember
Love doesn't have a language, they say
So I guess your name in any context can heal the pain away
It speaks to me softly every day
And with time, fades everyone's memory
But your name will always remind me of my identity

Pop

I smiled so hard
I might've popped.

Selfish

Call me selfish
You're not the first

Is it a crime
To ask for your hands
As though they were made only to mold the shape of my
body
To ask for your eyes
And promise to only start dreaming when they peer into
mine
To ask for your lips
Because they were meant to taste only me

Call me selfish
But am I not selfless

Tell me is it wrong
To offer you my heart
As though you are the only one worthy of my love
To give you every last inch of me
And promise to only ever let your hands wander me
To sacrifice all of my peace
Because your storm was meant to take complete control
over me

should we let our eyes talk for longer, or should we interrupt them to allow our lips to embrace?

Sore loser

I hate to lose
But if I have to lose, I'd rather it be to you
I hate the unknown
But if I had a blindfold, I'd follow you in the dark

I didn't need the reassurance
But somehow you know just what to say
I dislike sappy things
But your honey tastes the sweetest

I want to run the other direction
But your magnet pulls me back
I think about someone else
But no one else compares

I think you've said enough
But you continue to pester me
I think you're too sweet
But when I'm with you, I'm melting

I like a challenge
But you fight me just enough
I want that passion
But your electricity makes it easy

I'd like to leave
But something stops me every time
I don't want to stay
But I never want you to go

I hope I don't scare you
But you seem to take me like a champ
I can be a warning
But you'll venture through the storm

Simran Kalita

I think you want me
But I think I want you too
I hate losing
But I think I'm falling for you

Squiggle

He made me feel like a squiggle in a world full of straight
lines.
My body curved at every point where his fingers touched
me.

Look of Love/I Hate

Smiling for my camera even though you hate taking
pictures
Laughing at my jokes even though they aren't funny
Thinking I'm the best even though I'm always down
Liking all my poses even though I'm not a model
Telling me to eat even though I'm not hungry
Letting me shine even though you're shiny too

Talking like we're children, with our endless conversation
Sneaking sneaky looks, keep our real intentions hidden
Give me the look of love, when your eyes ask my soul a
question
My answer is your smile, the one where my eyes twinkle

I hate the way I only want to talk to you
I hate the way you always look at me like you're about to
say something
But you never do
I hate the way the gaze you give I know is the look of love,
but you stop yourself from saying it every time

I hate the way I can't find the words to express myself
I hate the way someone from the broken pieces of my past
is the reason why

I hate how I really do hate your laugh
I hate that your dancing is so embarrassing
I hate that you're materialistic & set in your dumb ways
I hate how that still doesn't make a difference

I hate how you never care to respond
I hate how you lock yourself in
I hate that you never bother to call
I hate that you never ask me on a date

I hate that despite all your flaws I still chose to choose you
I hate that I don't want to stop liking you
I hate that everything you do has a forest of reasons stacked
behind it
I hate that we both are too scared to admit & lose
everything we never had

For some reason you're the only one I always want to have
fun with
Unknotting our past, present, & future sitting across from
you
You feel like home
Let me vent to you my crazy inhibitions
And at the end of the day, you're still there

Pretending we can erase these feelings if we rewrite over
them
Connecting as though we've known each other for some
fragments from our past
Reaching out your hands to catch me, hoping to be caught
if you fall too
Falling into a steady pace where one subsides the other
We bathe under the moonlight

An addiction you can't help chasing
A boy who sees the sun in her
A girl who found Mr. right in Mr. wrong
A lot in common between the both of you
Tearing at the seams for one another

You are each other's dreams

Sit awake in the forest
Take a hotel adventure
Backseat of his car
Anywhere at all, really

Thinking every guy that talks to me has to be making a
move
Falling slowly but already all at once
Moonshine in your pocket as an excuse to come see me
Flickering through the haze when your body comes close

An enigma, a tipsy trembling
Your face is a cloud of smoke in a mirror of mine
Can we just kiss already?
I'm tired of confessing my love to my bedroom walls

And I know you can feel it too
Because you're scrambling for the right words, the right
moves
But I'll make it simple for you
I home you, with the look of love

We don't meet often
We don't cross paths
But something makes you feel like home
And I'm always with you, tonight

I wasn't religious until I crossed paths with you—
You're how I pray now.

The Softest Feeling

The greatest feeling was his arms wrapped around me like a
blanket over a child
The greatest feeling was his steady breath against my ear as
he ran his hands through my hair

The warmest feeling was the simple knowledge that he was
there and didn't want me gone
The wildest feeling was me falling head over heels even if
he hadn't

The saddest feeling is that all I have left is a lingering hope
that maybe you feel the same
And maybe we'll love just in time before you leave.

Love

I didn't know I had the capacity to love until you. I didn't know that this could explode within me and come seeping out relentlessly. Its powers such that it is directionless, limitless, with no reason. I just want him, that's all I want. I want him to be happy, I want him to never be upset. I want him to get through each day, even if it's with someone else. I could be your everything. I could love you and protect you because that's just how much love I have coming from inside me right now, despite the fact that, for him, I was just another passenger.

That's the crazy, funny thing about love. It hits you at 1 am while you're listening to a new old song and staring out the window, while you're supposed to be talking to someone but are unable to think about anything but him. My mind is filled with thoughts of you. Did you eat ok? Who do you talk to? Do you ever think of me? Do you think of me when you eat cannoli? What did you cook last night? Are you unhappy? Do you also get memories of me, the same way I get memories of you? Do you love me? Do you love me back with the same force, a full force worth a thousand trucks? Can you do anything for me? Sacrifice the man that you are for me? Could you marry me? I could marry you. I'm in love with you.

My poetry exists because you exist.

Our Souls at Night

Our souls at night
go for a walk.
It's very cold
but I hold you tight.

Because this is the only time
I can feel your body pressed against me.
And I will savor this moment forever

Until I wake up.

Simran Kalita

Under The Influence

Every time you pass me by,
I feel a certain way
my nose raises & my eyes close
Your scent is all I can think of
All I want to remember

Holding onto you is like holding onto sand
But I crave this addiction even in the midst
of your silence

Your shadow passes me and the way my body curves, oh
was that too much?
Yearning for you is like a habit of mine, a daily reminder
just like my pills
And I only grow stronger in my love for you

I'm now floating in a black pool of your love
A sea of onyx, as I wait
Picturing your figure and I turn into liquid gold
Melting to the floor and through your palms,
forever & ever

When I dance, I imagine you right next to me
Slowly and slowly and slowly but gently
Slip right next to me,
while we move to the moonlight

Scattered and shining like diamonds
We're on the horizon
Give me the crack of morning
As we stumble into each other

The Poet Inside Me

This fragrance, you're so divine
You are the heroin to my opioid,
the outer space I don't mind jumping into
We're free-falling now

A trail of you and your love runs across the veins of my
body
I'm happy
Captured and made slaves of the day
Only to find me in your dreams

The hunger grows restless in my belly
The thirst gets tempted in my throat
My own bodice taunts me in my shadows,
a reflection of what could be yours

It's like your body is laced
See what you do to me.

Simran Kalita

What Love Feels Like

It isn't telling her she's the hottest girl you've ever met
It's in the little glances, to make sure she's ok
in the midst of a crowd of strangers
And you hold each other's hands, tightly

It isn't the corny 'good morning' text
It's the text she gets as she's opening her front door
after getting back from dinner
on her weekly girls' night
Making sure she got home ok

It isn't the five-star restaurant you take her to every night
It's the spoon of soup you force her to eat
when she's sick and looks like a mess, but a cute mess
It's the comfort food you secretly order for her
while she complained on FaceTime what she was craving

It isn't the posting on social media and liking comments
It's taking a walk with her right before sunrise
because you spent the whole night up talking
And you can't take your eyes off her so you trip
in the middle of the road, again and again

It isn't having a girl you get to take home every night
It's the honor of having her to hold, to touch, to talk to
while she sits on your lap and looks at you with
big, meaningful eyes
It's her having you as an anchor of sanctity, sacred and her
own

It's the ice cream you get together at night
It's the work you put into making things right
It's wiping each other's tears away
It's always finding a reason to stay

It's the talking, the constant missing, the yearn
It's the heart's butterfly when you get her text
It's the partner whose hand you hold no matter what
It's the feeling that this person just *gets* you

It's not the wow, the amazing, the fantabulous
the flashy, the shiny, the boat loads of jewels
the ring, the roses, the boxes of chocolate
It's the ok

Love feels like ok, but you're ok forever.

Pinky promise

Promise me that you love me
Promise me that you're not lying
Promise me that the things you say come straight from your
heart
Promise me that you're mine
Promise me I'm the only one
Promise me for every lifetime
Promise me that it was always and will always be me
Promise me that you'll try

Your fragrance is my antidote.

Simran Kalita

Give Me Everything

Give me now
Give me today, give me tomorrow
Give me every fleeting moment

Give me life that soars out of you
Give me the sorrow we don't talk about
Give me fragments of a drawing board misaligned

Give me the breath that you're afraid to release
Give me the inching pain when you bite your lip
Give me the finger I use to peruse through the corners
Of your brain

Give me the nod of approval where you seal my skin
From the remnants of you
Give me the five dew drops that have formed at the bottom
Of your foggy window since I got here
Give me stars I'm seeing because your scent
Makes me so dizzy

Give me the truth written across your face
That I am too blind to read
Give me the pain I don't want it so take it back
Give me you if I can't have it then no one else can too.

The Poet Inside Me

Every move he makes is like a magnet that moves me too.

Simran Kalita

Like the First Time

I want every time we kiss to be like the first time
I want every time we lock eyes to be like the first hello

I want every time we laugh to be like the first joke
I want every time we hug to be like the first embrace

I want every time we talk to be like the first conversation
I want every time we confess to be like the first feeling

I want you to hold me like it was the first time I ever
Entered your arms
But as if it is the last time you'll be seeing me

I want to be able to look at you, and you know exactly what
I'm thinking
And you're thinking the same thing

I want you to love me every day like it was the first time.

You

Finding you is a gift
Choosing you is an inevitability
Keeping you is the string of my favorite-colored balloon
Having you is a balancing act on a tightrope
Losing you is a defeat with no recovery

Simran Kalita

Decisions

Do you feel me when I think of you?
Because the simple memory of your smile sends butterflies
down my

Do you always know just what to say?
The words you said and I interpreted a different way

What do you think about when you think of me?
Is there a reason why you're ignoring me?

My heart can't take another blister
Especially since you're all she thinks about since the day
you kissed her

Your hands are strong and waiting for me
But I will cease you happily

I can't take this silence, this heavy-hearted solace
Once I've tasted joy, it's hard to come back from that

I want to end this, but it's so hard to let go
You're everything I ever wanted, and maybe that's the joke

I'm tired of this back and forth
Can you just come over already?

I want so badly to run into your arms
But I'm so afraid you'll say no

Maybe, if only your return hadn't given me hope
Because right now I'd either be yours or live happily alone.

Deepness

I was going to sink anyway, but I chose your ocean.

Simran Kalita

Like the Leaves

You're running through my head
Pulling apart everything

You've been here before
You know the way you make me feel

Why are you so shy?
Why don't you pull me in?

You're not my everything
You're not my anything

I just want to kiss you
I just want to love you

Instead, I'm staring at the dead flowers
you got for me

Leave me alone
Whisper in my ear

Take the pain away
Let me know how you feel

I'm immortalized in your shadows
I'm everything in your dream world

Why don't you let dreams become your reality?
What are you afraid of?

Climb onto me
Cling to me

Is it fate that we're here together?
Why do you feel so familiar?

Take a leap of everlasting faith
I know you're worried, but I promise you you're safe

Why do we find ourselves here again?
Why can't I ignore you and play pretend?

The end is not the beginning
The beginning is coming to an end

Feel your way through me again
Free yourself of everything

Simran Kalita

"You're the closest to heaven that I'll ever be"

If I am the sun,
then why does it feel like you're the moon sleeping with all
the stars?

You put me above the clouds
So why do I feel earth at my toes
while you revolve in your commotion

You said I'm Eden
but wouldn't you want to be there all the time
instead of making a weekend trip to my hotel?

Shouldn't that make me home
when all the roads find me again?

If I'm the saint and you're the sinner
Shouldn't you come back to the steps of my temple to
repent?
I won't let you sleep with jezebel
no matter how perfect she may appear to be to you

I could protect you
I could save you,
save you from yourself
save you from Himself

If I'll ever see you again

'Cause when night falls,
you're on a whole other axis
and I'm wide awake

The Poet Inside Me

We're both alive at night
but for different reasons
I'm up for you
you're up for everything but me.

Come back to me once again.
Even though sun & moon don't meet
I'll escape to become one of your billion stars
If you choose me.

Films

I used to dream in black & white
With faceless people

You brought in screaming technicolor
A direction towards loving

Now, if you go, who's going to star in my nightly movies?

Cold November

Time stops, and it feels so good
Eyes hurt from staring at your every curve
Taking you in the way I drink my morning tea
To simply have you here is not enough

Cold fingers as they trace over the space between us
The air captures within it every moment of meaning
The air traps us in its unsparing transposition
I can feel your heart skip a beat as you step towards me

Why does time have to travel so slowly?
Why don't I feel it's on my side?
When night comes, and you're not here
Will there ever be a time when you'll be here?

I fight my way against the wind
Trying so hard to feel your lips
Don't look at me the way you are right now
Watch me crumble as you take a pause

When all the souls around us start to dim their light
And the only candle glowing is yours so bright
I will follow you through your forest
I will ride until tomorrow

Go through and open every single one of my doors
Lift the curtains to let the windows bring sun in
Call my lovers and tell them it's over
I am now yours forever

Use your fingers to carve my shape
The way your hands feel takes my breath away
You're cold November, and I'm warm summer
You light my ocean on fire

Simran Kalita

Feel me moan as we collapse into each other
When the world is quiet, you carefully whisper
Breathe me in, let your desires play out
When you were gone, this desert was in a drought

But now you're where you're meant to be
Under my gaze and happily
Let time take its time bringing you to me
One day, we'll be under the covers fast asleep

Pulse

And everything comes down
To this
Very
Moment

.

Simran Kalita

Sleep

I know you were awake.

Spending extra minutes in bed together
Creeping up closer to you just so I could feel you breathing
Raising a hand to place it on your shoulder
just so you could push it off and move closer

You didn't want me to see you because you
thought I didn't want you to see me
How wrong could you be

Now my bedsheets still smell like you
And I didn't wash them until the last remnants
of you were gone

Watching each other lay there, in our messy outerwear
A dance we danced so delicately
So not to let the other know we aren't asleep

I wish I never put those pillows up between us
I wish I just ran to you, I wish I melted in your embrace

We're restless in the morning, so close but so far
Not touching, but at the same time, wrapped up in each
other's
presence
Are we not going to talk about it?

My hair all disheveled, my puffy skin in the morning
Bodies long and curved into each other, don't touch
Your pants unzipped, hands under your shirt
Knees raised, hair all over your face

Morning came way too soon,
what happened at night?
after I picked you up, tucked you in
Brought you to my bed

I watched you climb out of the darkest place,
was there when you couldn't show me your face
But I was always there

Thinking about your piercing gaze
While I refused to lock eyes with you
Waiting for all my friends to leave
Getting frustrated that I wasn't getting it

I didn't want to be your one-night escape

How did it feel to sleep with me, just sleep
Did I try to cuddle, did I whisper your name
Because my roommate said I do
When every night I dream of you

How did it feel to feel the crushing blow of my rejection
Not knowing that I was just way too confused to make
my brain make sense
Watching you with another girl the whole night
I didn't realize that you still wanted me

I wore the PJ's you bought me for my birthday,
just like you asked me to
You saw them when I carried you to bed,
waited for you in my bathroom
in the morning before you left
Only to forget that you even got me a gift
a couple days later

Simran Kalita

Is this the retaliation I get
for not kissing you in my bed
for not sitting next to you on the couch
for staying a distance away, just like you said
I thought you didn't want me anymore
So why are we both hurt?

We were lying in my bed, being closer than comfortable
It felt like routine
Until you needed to leave
Can you not get that my head was messed up, I was fryed

Just to be close to you was enough for me
Inching closer and closer until your alarm rang
You could've put your arm around me, I wish
you did

I'm smooth like butter with every guy that I meet
But with you there's a heat
And it's burning my insides
I get too nervous to call you mine
I wish you were mine

I wanted to call you to apologize
But you never let me get a word in
Were you embarrassed? Don't be

How did it feel to see me in the morning?
To realize we woke up with each other
On my twentieth birthday
A girl doesn't forget a night like that

Your hand in my hair, your words before I left to change
Watching me in bed with you
Laughing at jokes only we knew
Everyone could tell you were going to stay the night

I know you wanted me
I just couldn't bring myself to tell you
I wanted you too
I thought we had more time
I thought I could make things right
And now you'll be two thousand miles away
And we both spend time with other people
Can't even find sleep some nights
I went out with another guy,
the very night after I saw you a week and a half later
Why was it so hard for us to meet?
Why are there so many things in between
And we won't even get to talk about them

Maybe it wasn't meant to be
My brother told me if someone doesn't change for you
clearly you're not the one he's supposed to change for
And that brought me to my knees

Experiencing a heartbreak that you never even asked for
I thought you'd be my comfort
solace, peace
I thought you were home
Why am I tearing my sheets apart, crying in the middle of
my bed
Because you never replied to the texts I sent

I thought you'd be different
You took me down a spiral staircase,
a fall much more painful than all the ones I've climbed
before
I'm dead before the last step

But remembering you in my bed, waiting for me
Remembering us by the trees, by the pond, by the bunnies
Us by the sea, getting drunk at dinner, talking in my
apartment
Leaving at 4 am, waking up at 9 am, calling till 12 am
It does something to a girl

Did you never feel the same?
Or am I clearly just insane
I fall too hard for the wrong guy,
I'm a sap for your smile
And now I say goodbye

I know your deepest, darkest secrets, your very best friend
Make promises to me that you can't keep
Send a novel of love & tears
Like I've known you for years
To be a stranger at dinner the night before you leave

I can't bring myself to leave because

I know you were awake.

How faithful

How faithful are these eyes
That look no further than your shadow
How faithful are these hands
That stay firmly within my own pockets
How faithful are my dreams
That invite no new guests even long after you leave

Simran Kalita

The words we haven't said

Everywhere I go
I see you in every face
I can't live without you
But I want to
It seems too hard for me to breathe

So close to saying the words
They're spilling out now
But they are carefully masked behind
The things we say we don't mean

And I tell you I hate you
And you tell me I frustrate you
It's getting harder for me to breathe

She wants to fix us soon
Prays we'll see the light
Wants you to tell me how you feel

The words we try to say
Get crushed by our mistakes
The heartbeats in my room
You know they yearn for you
We both can't get up off our
High horses

So hold me tight tonight
Pretend it's just a usual fight
Like the sky is blue everyday
And that we'll both stay

The words I want to say
And you've told me when I was asleep
Fall from the place they had risen from

My heart
It begs for me to tell you
And I know what this silly guy wants
I can't control it anymore
It wants you.

Only you, all I ask for is you.

These hands, these lips,
these eyes, this smile,
your hair, the way you make me feel
on a warm summer's night.

I go crazy for you, baby. Running
my hands through your mop of hair…
Disheveled and about to nip at me
I run.

You dissolve me into your hands, as I
crumble I'm scattered. Torn apart and
waiting just for you every day.

You're a miracle, and I'm crazy about you.
Crazy.

Simran Kalita

All my love

My love is laced up in a small white pouch
With silk golden strings knotted together
Enclosing my heart's woes

I leave it here for you

The upper corners of my back are fastened to a string
You'd mistake it for a butterfly's wings
But really, I'm tied to the hands of my puppeteer

I'm leaving here for you

All my love, all my life
Happened so fast I never took a moment to take a breath, to
take a step
Forward, or maybe even backward
How lovely would it be falling backwards with you

Letting myself entertain the world, appear so noble
When backstage I'm no different than a jester, I'm just
prettier

All my love, I'm leaving only for you

When we meet each other in our dreams, do you think you'll still be happy to see me?

Simran Kalita

Glass house

To think of what might've been
If we both knew the right words
To think of the possibilities
If you were right in front of me

I've been waiting for a sign
So everything points me to you
This loving was not satisfied
So come back for a round or two

If you let me love you
I would love you so carefully
If you let me have you
I'd have you in every corner of our mansion

Can we build a glass house?
Because I can see from the way you're looking at me
That if we filled a glass house
We'd need nothing more than just you and me

All the pain that you put me through
You promise it was just a side effect of my disbelief?
Nothing you would do on purpose
'Cause my baby was only looking out for me

Oh, I think everything's a sign
So I keep on choosing you
You asked me not to wait
But you taste just like my favorite addiction

If you let me touch you
I'd play with the strings in your heart
If you let me call you
I'd call you every word that replaces love

Can we build a glass house?
Because I can see from the way you're looking at me
That if we filled a glass house
We'd need nothing more than just you and me

And when we build our glass house
Every room would have a memory
'Cause if we had a glass house
I'd know just what you're thinking

I tried and I tried
For three whole fucking summers
But the thoughts of you
Don't seem to listen

The doubts that I had all resurfaced
And my friends are telling me you're long gone
But how can I forget
What you told your friends about me

Didn't think I'd have to lose you
Don't think we can be just friends
Am I the only one who's spinning
From the cracks of our mess

I'd love to build a glass house
Where it would be just you and me
And everyone's invited
'Cause with you, life's a party

Can we build a glass house?
Because I can see from the way you're looking at me
That if we filled a glass house
We'd need nothing more than just you and me

Truth

There have been many before you,
and there will be many after
But you were the first
who made me feel a type of way
That one can't describe with words
That one can only describe with fingertips
Tracing across each other, ever so gently
Feeling the atmosphere push and pull apart
In the slightest

You were my first
Not the first to hold me
Not the first to baffle me
Not the first to hurt me
You were my first love

And I'd give a thousand more promises
to a thousand more lovers
If it meant I'd be with you for a moment longer

Your hair, your lips, your smile
Not a word can slip from your tongue
to make me think you are anything but carved of gold

Not a thousand gashes from the words you couldn't say
could make me hate you any more or love you any less
You were my everything

And though time will eventually let me win this war
I promise not to forget you

Though it seems like the river that flows between us
Has made a valley so big that I would drown if I did
venture
But even if all the world's echoes told me not to see you
I'd still turn around to sneak a glance

I love you
I love you
I love you

Backbone

I want you here,
not because of any other reason
but because I want *you* here

I want your encouragement,
not because others don't encourage me
but because I want *you* to be happy for me

I want your support,
not because I have nobody's support
but because I wanted *your* approval

I want your hand to rest on my shoulder,
not because I miss your touch
but because it comforts me to feel home in your fingers

I wanted you there,
to be here always,
and I will continue to want you to be here,
not because it makes a difference that you're not
but because

I stand a little taller knowing you're next to me
I smile a little cheesier hearing you laugh at my joke
My tears dry a little quicker because you're wiping them
away
My hands sweat a little less hearing your reassuring words
The pain feels a little easier to endure since you want me to
heal
I love a little harder because it's you I'm loving

I wish you could be my backbone
because I'm crumbling without you.

Loving is Oblivion

Loving is a love affair that we deny ourselves of much too often. What is wrong in it ? What do you fault with it ? Why can't I be happy ? Why can't I ask for too much ? Oh, is too much too much to ask for ?

Loving is a love affair where both of us are gagged and tied side by side. We have black scarves over our eyes. Oh, I can't see your pretty blue ones. We scream into the unknown. We scream into each other. We scream at each other. Both of us are alone and shattered, yet we are together and helpless. What a pair are we.

Loving is a love affair where all turns into fire. And, honey, if you haven't felt that yet, then I'm sorry that you haven't felt desire.

Simran Kalita

True Love

My dad will never miss my call
My brother will scoff at anyone he thinks remotely isn't
good to me
My mom only makes my favorite foods
My dog competes with me for my mom but lays his head
on my lap at night

I learned Spanish to speak with a two-year-old at work
I am prepared to sucker punch any asshole that will mess
with my younger cousin
I give the tightest hugs to people even when they don't
need it

Love is not perfect
But love is not a tragedy

I used to believe love had to be perfect
It had to be this exact person because he fills these exact
requirements
Love is in the moments where you find yourself doing
something that means more than just yourself
Love is an action that, somewhere in this universe, creates a
binding contract between two souls

I sure want to see you up there when we all kick it
Read that again in the old pirate from Spongebob's voice
Love is saying I hope this isn't the end of our story
You're pretty awesome

When people are not perfect
How can we expect love to be perfect
It's messy, and you try to wrap your hands around it
But it's quick

You have to be careful
It's hard to capture love
But once you have it, treasure it
It chose you, too

I don't know if I can say that I've loved before
The concept is so foreign to me
But if I find myself never wanting to lose someone
And I have, then maybe that's getting close

Simran Kalita

Love Letter

(This poem is for my children, the ones I saw every day at the school I worked at. My love for each one of you is immeasurable, unconditional, and never-ending.)

My, my butterfly
I watch as you look up at the sky
Your pretty eyes with so many questions
My curiosity to know what you're thinking
So many emotions fleet across your face

Your every sigh is a new adventure
You're hungry for the future, but slow down, my love
Your little giggle is my heart's favorite sound
Your familiar habits give my mind endless possibilities as to who you will become

I hope you never lose your spirit
There are so many things I wish I could say to you
Instead of goodbye
I wish I could be with you every moment to know what goes on through your head

Are you happy? Are you tired?
What makes you sad?
Do you feel that someone doesn't love you enough?
You're much too young to ever have problems, and although it is pointless for me to hope, I hope you never do
I dream of a perfect world for you

All I can give you is my protection
My endless blessings—that is my devotion
Your eyes are what make every day worth living, hoping that what you see is better than what this world can give
You are my dreams come true, and I will always miss you.

One thing was certain from the moment we met:
I would find you in every lifetime.

Unrequited Love

There's something absolutely beautiful
about unrequited love
Because all it is is passion
Burning hot, fiery passion
And there's no control
But what is there to control
When love simply falls out of you
And grapples everything it touches
With its grip

There's something magical about
unrequited love
Something that makes tears look beautiful
And sobs seem like cries of joy
Even the yearning for your love becomes
an everyday task
It's not something that many people enjoy
But I think that

There's something absolutely mad and
crazy and insane about unrequited love
It's a great hunger
That one can only dream of tasting
However with the satisfaction
Of knowing that there will forever be a
beautiful dream
Will rest assure them a peaceful slumber
Because their wild and unrequited love will
only be so much greater if it were a possibility.

I know I still give you butterflies.

Milk & Honey

It's sacred, it's fragile, it's holy.
It's mine.
Its rights are mine.
Its eyes are mine and mine alone.

You don't have any say on which direction the wind blows
the leaves
Nor the bellowing enormity of the sea waves,
So why do you believe that you can have a say on the most
uncontrollable feeling.

It's got me completely in its fingertips.
Entangled and surrendered to the most organic state of
mind.
I lie awake at night.

And the pain that it causes me at the very core of my
system
Will never compare to the cliche butterflies that swarm
around in my belly.
But is it really honeybees.

Because your love is so sickly sweet and its drops drip
from my fingers.
And yet you sting me from the inside out.

But I do not regret any decision I have made when it comes
to stumbling into love with you
All these reasons brought me to you in the first place.

And a world without you is a world without the soft milk or
fur to lose yourself in.

Checklist

You cannot imagine your life before them

You do not want to imagine a life after them

As if you have always known them

When you want them to be the first to hear your news

And they know what you are about to say

You know what would hurt them

They know what would hurt you

But you both would never hurt each other

You didn't need to meet them more than twice to call them
a friend

You feel home with them a thousand miles away from
comfort

They've been there for you every step of your way

Looking into their eyes feels so strong you are forced to
look away

While sitting across from them, the thought comes to mind
"They would do anything"

The perfect puzzle piece you didn't know was missing

You would find each other at the end of the night

Among others, you would always want their touch—
tomorrow or in forty years

One day, you will wake up beside each other

No matter what they are doing, you would have them

It would be earth-shattering

Their smell electrocutes you

Their eyes entrance you

Confiding in them your deepest darkest secrets is easy

But they seem to have already known and accepted your
flaws

Hiding from them is futile

Running to them is second nature

In your dreams, you find yourself in their presence

A day without them is tolerable but mimics a sky with no
stars

To fall into them is to fall for your best friend

The key to your lock

Why can I read all your thoughts?

Your memories sound like my past

Their name guarantees your smile

No matter the years, I'll hold your hand

You were meant for me

I was meant for you

Their weakness makes you vigilant

Your weakness does not exist to them

Life goes on without them, but with them, it's a never-ending adventure

Why do all the motifs point to you?

I have waited for you all my life

The nighttime is the hardest

Their aura brings you peace

One day, one night may be enough, but you chase the one lifetime

I can't believe you have been alive this whole time

Are you really meant for me?

The earth may have stars, but her stars shine brighter in your eyes

Your memory lives on forever

Every moment is enough; a conversation seals the hurricane

Fall here or fall there, I hope I land in your arms

You've got me

Why must you control my every movement?

Happy for your every success

Crying at the club because I miss you

I don't want to lose you, even if it means we lose each other

We might be the last two left in this place

Take my hand; you'll always be safe

Laugh at all my inside jokes

Every prayer has your name

My reflection looks happier to me with you standing in my mirror

Drink poison; your name is my last

I want someone to think I put the stars in their sky.

Him

Simran Kalita

Which part of you should I keep—the one I loved or the one that told me to leave?

The Poet Inside Me

Unopened promises

Why would you promise me the moon
If you can't afford one of her stars

Why would you vow to take me to the ocean
If her sea waves disrupt you

Why would you gift me the necklace of time
When you're never here

Why would you look me in the eyes
If you only see what you want to

Why wouldn't you see reason
When I tell you the truth

Why do you trust your brain
When your heart lies with me

Why do you live in chaos
When my aura brings you peace

Why would you choose to love me
And still leave me

Why do you lie awake at night
When you could sleep with me

Why do you waste your breath
When you could spend hours pouring into me

Why would you come back
If you didn't even reach out to me

Simran Kalita

Why would you want me
If you didn't want to be with me

Why would you still keep me
If you didn't always need me

Why would you throw me away
When I'm the only one who can ease the pain

Him.

I'm still not over his laugh
His smile that would split his face in half
His brown eyes with specks of green and gold
His throaty chuckle
His cold sticky hands
The curl of golden hair above his eyes
The way he'd look at me from the side
His perfectly crafted brows
The way he would tower over me but still be close
His soft low voice
His stories
The way he would get excited, so childlike
The things he'd tell me
His shyness
His curiosity
The way he opened the door for me
Him holding the box when it was cold
His nervous playfulness
His rebellious tricks
His respectability
His quiet joking
His quick movements
His goofiness

He's not the god I portray him to be
He has flaws and many at that
But for me he was fine
I thought that if I tried harder, fought harder, he would stay
I thought I'd be more than perfect for him
I thought he'd fill the empty spaces and crevices I couldn't
reach around
I thought I'd show him a new perspective

I guess I was wrong. I don't know if it was meant to be for us not to be or if it's still meant to be. I just know I liked spending time with him. Eating cannoli. talking about life. being nervous and awkward and shy, making all the wrong moves at the right time.

Maybe if I had let it go on longer, I would've caught myself slipping more and more into the dark abyss of his love. But what I found by taking a leap of faith was that the pool was empty. And so I was left hitting concrete hard and head on. Dead. My blood pooled out as I lay there arms and legs flailed, staring up at his eyes as he peered down at me, curious and unknowing of it all.

I do doubt myself. Was it ever even there? Did I see what was naked to everyone else? Am I losing my own mind? He's so different. Maybe I'm just unlucky. Maybe it just wasn't meant to be. I give up

Why

I'm still going to remember that night
Where it felt like we were the only two people left in this
world
And we buried into each other the secrets we never thought
anyone would learn
I still think about that night

I still remember the way we walked all the way to my place
And you followed my every movement so gently, noticed
the way I stood beside you
I can't erase those memories

Talking about the things that annoy us, what fascinates us
Feeling the world come together to stay silent just for us to
be alone
I don't think it was a coincidence that we felt electricity
without touch

A never-ending love story that I can't seem to replace
A way that my body senses exactly what goes on in your
brain
You can keep me in a ballerina box so I can dance with you

I am so stuck on those memories
I remember the bunnies
We melted into each other, and things were so familiar

Why can't it be this way
Where I make you stay
Where you choose to stay

Why couldn't you call
Why couldn't you even text back
I just wanted to see you one last time

Why did you have to make me believe once again that
something was there
And every time you give me hope
But then you're in bed with a nameless someone else
instead

Why wasn't I enough to make you change your ways
It's not fair being put on a pedestal
I'm lonely all the way up here
You don't even care

I can't understand Why things had to be this way.

Forbidden

So it was real
All of it
Every moment of it
It wasn't just in my head

I'm sorry
Is the words I try to keep in my head
Repeating till I believe them
Not sure how to make sense of them

Why
Oh why
Did this happen to me
To us

You were there
And I was there
And it was so simple
I'm lost alone now

Floating creatures in our sea of tonic
Lying helpless in the crashing waves
How could I have been so blind
Why couldn't I just see fate

Let the wind consume you
Let the light pursue you
Let your words free you
This regret will eat you up alive

Surrender

Why can't you look at me
Why can't I be the one
that saves you

Why couldn't we let it go
Instead of keeping our lips sealed
Escaping from our reality,
from our future

Why couldn't we call the spade a spade
The sun our light
Our glances our love
Our love our love

Now I'm screaming crying
clutching for something
that disappeared the moment I went home

You wanted to see me
The way I wanted to see you
Instead we looked away

I'm wrapped up around your finger
Tired from the battle
but still lost at sea
still hopelessly
in love with you

"Don't forget about me"
Please don't forget about me?
How could I forget about you
How can't I care about you
I don't have it in me

The Poet Inside Me

I wish I was your escape
I wish I wasn't what you escaped
I wish you wanted me more
but I wish you wanted you more

You're wrapped up in your own head
You're the prisoner, your own guard
Why is it so hard
To keep our love from spilling onto the pages

Fighting, falling, grasping, not calling
Life is life is love is sour
Bittersweet memories
You wanted me, you ran for free

Passing notes, kindergarten haze
I wish that was our reel
Instead we're crossing mountains,
building bridges, slipping farther

Tongue-tied until we weren't
Flying high until we're sober
Caught a vibe and now it's over

I still love you
I'll still love you
I'm still here
I'm always here

Saying the right words even though
you won't say anything at all

I'm tired, restless
I know you made me understand
But I don't want to
I loved you

Simran Kalita

I see no reason
Not when you're there
I'm here
We're free
Birds that fly high
Until you were captured

I set you free
But you're not with me
You're in shackles in your own mind
What's the matter
Why can't you let me in
Let me be your escape

I did it once, I can do it again
The motto that pulses through my veins
But you're halfway insane
Making promises you can't keep
Making promises to me
Why are you making promises to me?

Let me wrap you in my love
We're floating above
Call out for me, anytime
I miss you in the night sky
I miss you all the time

There's no point explaining things to me
I won't see reason
The way you won't see me
Don't hide yourself from me please
I love you

So many moons ago
We stood talking our hearts away
Keeping them hidden behind our chests
When they beat for each other
Do you really not feel that way anymore?

How can you let a feeling like that vanish
So suddenly
Especially when you know now I was always there
Crying, sulking, smiling, wondering
Always there

I lie and I pretend
But I am always here
So come now to me
I will accept you for who you are
It's who I fell in love with
My personal golden boy

You won't let me see
The scars that cover your body
The demons that plague your mind
I'm always here with you still, tonight

Simran Kalita

Gone

And I probably don't even cross your mind
When you cross the street without looking at the sign
When you run your hand through another's hair
The way you did while we were sleeping

And you probably forgot about what we had
When all the world came silent for just us two
Freezing in the winter of Boston by the sea
Never did I think a boy could make me so happy

And I probably mean nothing to you at all
When you were the only best friend I wanted to call
The only person who understood what I felt
You redefined home

Now we're strangers
Strangers
Strangers walking past each other on the street
Do you have another life? One that I am not a part of

Am I just a memory
Or do you still consider me
Where do I lie, buried deep in the confines of your head
I always said you had ugly hair
Oh, The things that could've been

I keep asking questions that will never be answered.

Don't

Don't tell me you love me
if you don't

Don't tell me you dream of me
if you've never dreamt before

Don't tell me everyone you love would love me
if they've never met me

Don't tell me things will get better
if they won't

Don't give me false promises that you'll think of me
if you won't even reach out

Don't let me believe that despite all this you still love me
if you don't even text back

Don't tell me you don't have anyone to talk to
when I wanted to talk to you, but you didn't care

Don't tell me you never saw this coming
if you really believe this

Don't tell me that you're surprised you had me right where
you could've wanted me, standing there telling you I love
you, expecting you to love me back
if you were ever there

Don't toy with my heart
I'm not that durable

Don't listen to my songs
they're all about you

The Poet Inside Me

Don't try to text me to get my attention
because you know it'll work

Don't spend endless conversations getting to know each
other putting our puzzle pieces together
if you know we won't fit

Don't pretend you care
when you don't

Don't keep the truth from me
it's the same thing as lying

Don't hide yourself from me
I thought we were more than this

Don't build me up, parade me around, admire me from up
close
only to throw me away from afar

Don't spend long hours at night with me
if you don't want to see me

Don't let me wear your jacket
if you're feeling cold

Don't follow me at my every step
if you don't want to hold me

Don't tell me you'll listen to me cry
if you'll forget we had plans

Don't ask me to come over today tomorrow the day after
anytime
if we never meet

Simran Kalita

Don't break my heart
I'm already a crier

Don't look at me like you're holding onto every word I say
if you're going back home alone

Don't tell me about the things that have beat you down
when we won't even get to talk about them

Don't be surprised that we click so easily
Don't come near me when I'm angry
Don't even think about asking me about myself
if you truly don't need me the way I need you

Don't tell me I have a beautiful mind and soul
if you won't tell me I look beautiful tonight

Don't comment on my pictures
if you're liking another girl's photos

Don't frame the poem I wrote for you
when you haven't heard all of them

Don't keep my souvenirs
when you keep breaking them

Don't even talk to me
if you don't want to facetime for hours

Don't stand with me in the garden in the courtyard on the
steps by the bunnies near the koi fish chasing my bike
around our campus by my building on the boat
if you're not going to kiss me

Don't give me hope
when you would rather occupy your mind with every other
thought

Don't tell me things that make me think you're trying to
say something else
if you didn't think before speaking

Don't give me excuses
if that's all you know to do

Don't jump up and down
when you're not that excited

Don't even message me
until you feel like replying

Don't love me
and let me believe it

Simran Kalita

Stereo Nights and Xbox Games that Betray

It's a game isn't it
And I can never win
It's a joke I realized
You hide it well in your eyes
Almost had me disbelieving

And you told me that you want me
But you really don't want me that much
You told me that you need me
You told me that you'd breathe me
Then you blew me out

And I can't do this anymore
I can't love without loving you
You don't seem to understand
Someone took my hand
And it will never be you again

Your touch I can still remember
Hold me close but not close enough
Something that I got used to after a while

You told me that you love me
Only for it all to get ugly right after
You told me that you love me
And ran away with blondie when we were done

None of it meant anything to me.

Death Wish

May you never stay up through the night enjoying endless
conversation
May her eyes never capture the depth of the raging sea nor
the secrets of the universe in a single blink
May her fragrance remind you of the sweetness that
could've once been yours to submerge yourself in

May you never feel that you could bury all your unhealthy
secrets into one person again
May you never feel like you can lie down and sleep next to
her forever
May her touch never thrill you with goosebumps because
she touched your soul

May her hair never hold within it the flow of the wind and
the softness of a stream
May your heart never flutter by simply staring at her in her
perfection
May she never feel whole sitting by you, just to breathe
next to you

May you never regain the strength to crawl up from the
depths of your despair
May your heart never fall in love again
May the scars from my body, brain, and heart hold as proof
of the poison you are capable of turning passion into

May you never feel the madness, and if you do, may you go
mad in your memories of what you lost with me
May your breath fall a little shorter, your chest feel a little
heavier knowing the sight of me is lost forever
May her soul never fully capture yours

May you never hold a lover in your arms again
May she never be enough to fill the void of joy I easily
spread with my wings
May your galaxy fall to emptiness and darkness without me

May the stars refuse to shine without my brightness
May your mornings feel the same as the nighttime
May you never feel intoxicated by simply the presence of
another, and if you do, may you stay intoxicated and
paralyzed in a corner, shaking from the aftershocks of me

May her laughter never fully allow your smile to bloom the
way it did for me, as if you lost your heart unwillingly
May you look into her eyes, knowing every part of your
soul will forever be searching for me
May you never feel the ease of a simple love affair

May a single lie turn into decades of betrayal
May her voice never put your ocean to sleep
May you listen to mine as a reminder on the days you miss
me, so every single day

May you brokenly accept that your heart has been lost to
me
May you piece together that your soul belongs with me
May you never wake up with an angel from heaven
sleeping next to you

May her touch never cause a thousand hurricanes to wash
all over your face
May her body never curve the same way mine did for you
May her lips never taste the way mine promised to you

May you cry every day
May not a single moment pass by where you don't miss the
sound of my heartbeat
May every person in your life abandon you the way you
ended the story of me

May you never feel friendship
May you never seek comfort
May you never receive a drop of happiness the way it came
so flowingly with me

May her heart never fully be yours
May you never want it the way you rose to claim mine
May every intimate moment feel like a redefining lie

May time cease to pass you by
May it never show you the mercy of erasing me
May you stay lost in my memory forever

May you never come close to hurting another
May my love turn into the dagger that stays lodged in your
heart, putting your whole life's end to my name
May you never find another who will love you and accept
you so willingly the way that I did

May no one, no thing, no place ever be enough to escape or
hide from what you did with me
May not a single moment of happiness allow you to forget
the euphoria you felt with me
May you finally understand the way you have lost your
heart mind body and soul to me

May her smile never allow you to forget me
May my music be a constant reminder
May my eyes remain locked and branded into every corner
of your brain

May I be the end the beginning the very essence of what
your soul craves, night and day
May the nighttime come like a wave of the things we did
together
May you never forget me, always live with the regret of
what you did to me

May you never feel our fire with another
May you never ever desire another
May you only love me forever

May you one day finally return to me

Loving you

Missing the way it felt
When life wasn't boring
Trying to capture that moment with someone else
As if it wasn't burned in my brain, your smile
Tracing lines where someone else had touched
All the times I wished it was you instead
Crying from the agony because I still wanted you
But you're dead to me
Following a ghost
You were never really here
Floating through life chasing your shadow
Letting the wind sweep me any direction
Where are you
Where did you go
When we were finally happy
Feeling everything inside me turn empty
We will never be
Hoping the clouds move past to bring you back to me
How can this be so ugly
With not a single person's faith in me
I see something in light
I see something in you
But my eyes follow blindly like a prophet
I only cause divide
I only cause pain
Whether it's you and me or the ones around us
There's no one like us
There's no one like us
I wish this upon no one

When will my tears ever stop?

Empty

They tell me every time
It hurts a little less
What they don't know
Is my heart breaks more and more
And it's overflowing

A love with no touch
No words
No identities
No thing to hold

A touch with no love
No warmth
No heartbeat
No eyes to lose myself in

Every hand that holds another
Every heart that loves another
Every word that shatters hope
Every tear that still waits for you to come home

You never do
You never do

I loved you first

I held you tight
Because I didn't want to let go
And the cars that pass me by
Cover the path that you rode

You probably forgot about me
How we stayed up late at night
Watching Friends all over again

You probably don't recall
The way you'd catch me when I'd fall

I've tried to start again but
There's more to moving on
Than just moving away

You probably have a family now
A big house, a dog, and a picket fence
Does your wife lean in the same way I did?

There's nothing to remember about me
Even when we pretended to marry

B

I wish you loved yourself enough
to love me too

I wish her hands roaming you
made you remember how much you wish they were mine

I wish you could fall out of my head
be better if I was dead

Nothing

At the end, there was nothing
Not a commotion
A sea of silence
No waves left to crash

And I should've known
I was stranded
Amidst the calm ocean around me
My own naivety echoing through the halls of my mind

I never asked for a birthday cake
I didn't ask for the moon or the stars
No shiny crystals or strings of pearl
I just asked to be noticed

Was it so much for me to ask?

Not a whisper to say I look beautiful tonight
Not a text to make sure I got home ok
Not a breath to release before kissing me
Not even an I love you

I didn't ask for any of it, so I got nothing

Simran Kalita

Changes

Holy luminescent tears
That cry still, relentlessly

Piles of crap I need to deal with
Time and time that keeps slipping

Headrush from the moment
Life's better on the other side of your mind

Balloons, wine, forget about it
Shit I gotta deal with

But every memory of you on repeat
The smell of your every inch lingering

My brain knows nothing
My heart is as stupid as they come

Is my life on pause?
Or am I too lazy to hit play

Let them fade
Let it fade

Betrayal

A thousand different ways to say I love you
But the only one I got was written in an apology

No tears left to cry

Crossing the bridge
I'd rather jump from it

You used to be pinned right next to my dad
I don't even know where you are anymore

Lonely nights that make me want to end it all
I'm the only one feeling this way

To everyone, I'm hopeless
A loser you made me into

Another one bites the dust
A new notch on my heartbreak belt

Falling in and out and in to love with you
I have a head rush, I'm bleeding

Throwing up from all the betrayal
Questioning why what what could have been different

You make me weak, I have lost it all
Not a single ounce of hope or faith or love left in me

Dried me out from the outside
Never let me come inside

What goes on in your filled up brain?
Whose posters do you board up in there

I'm drowning
Tears I cried for you are a river

There are none left now
I'm buried alive

Simran Kalita

Death

After you, a part of me died that loved easily
A part of me died that gave in abundance
A part of me died that believed in second chances

Meeting you, a part of me died that never thought I was
worth it
A part of me died that didn't love home
A part of me died that kept the little girl in me hidden &
locked away

Because of you, a part of me died that believed in true,
hopeless love
A part of me died that loved to have endless conversation
A part of me died that thought it would only be with you

Burying you, a part of me died that wanted more out of life
A part of me died that held onto every word you said
A part of me died that worried whether you got home
everyday

Mourning you, a part of me died that craves that feeling at
the core of my tummy
A part of me died that kept listening to the same voices
telling me I'm not enough
A part of me died that only received looks of pity and
sympathy

Before you, a part of me died that thought love could only
feel good
A part of me died that believed I could be good enough
A part of me died, leaving me worried for who I'd be with
you

Seeing you, a part of me died that knew hope
A part of me died that wondered if you were searching for
me too
A part of me died that believed till the end that there was a
meaning behind all this

But crashing into you, a part of me died that will ever love
again
A part of me died that wants to love again
A part of me died that will never stop loving you

.

It's hard to breathe because every song I wrote was about
you
Every love song has phrases that remind me of you
I know all this useless information like why you love your
mom so much, how you got that scar on your hand
Pieces of the personal puzzle I made of you
And now I just have to pretend like that ghost of you
doesn't exist
I have to turn my back on all the memories I have of you,
of us
I have to read the notes I wrote about you, listen to the
voice messages I saved talking about you and act like it
means nothing to me
It meant everything to me, but you weren't there
A part of me wishes I had never known you
Another part of me wishes I had met you a long time before
Or met you in the future when we were both strangers
wanting more
Would you have fought for me the way you don't now
The last bits of my feelings for you are seeming to
evaporate, but god knows the moment I see you they'll all
come fluttering back
And I can't decide if I want that again or not
Cause dying of your sickness is not something I'd wish
upon anyone
But I'd take that death happily myself
Waiting for a sign from you is like asking time to turn back
But I can never get sick of the conversations we had, the
moments we shared
So I'll just have to carry myself in the way that I do.

Poem

My day used to be incomplete
without thinking of you

At night I would lie awake hoping to
dream of you

I'd pretend you were missing me
the way I was missing you

But you never miss me at all

A simple look and I melted away,
imagining us

Praying for a sign, holding onto what
I thought were your moves

But your rhythm can't hear
my heartbeat

The way that I know if you asked,
I would stay

But I need to go

Moving on

It hurts because now I know you can live without me
Now I know you can breathe without me
Now I know I'm not needed

It hurts because now I know I'm not the only wish you
prayed to god for
Now I know you never even asked for me
Now I know you can forget me easily

I'm feeding myself excuses
Letting myself keep you alive replaying the fantasies of
you and I in my head
When I deserved more
Always

It hurts because every time I think I've moved on
I'm right back there, waiting for you to turn your head back
to look at me
Why don't you ever look at me

Eyes on the prize
Hand over your heart
Let me breathe
Your work of art

The stars & the moon & the milky way love to entertain me
Keep me from closing my eyes in the warm moonlight
To dream of you

But my mind knows to play the tricks
And now I see you even with my eyes wide open
A rewinding memory of our times together

Broken but still playing
I wrote every song about you
You danced to my rhythm

I'm over this hill
Up another mountain
Climbing and climbing, I've lost all air

Breathe me out
Don't let me in
Let me swim out of your trenches

I'm drowning in this sea of you
Calling out to anyone, anything
Take me off life support

Why does this happen every time
Why am I such a fool
Why can't my heart be loved

I'm just asking to be loved
And if I can't have you
I want to move on

Lullaby

I've had so many sleepless nights, watching the stars across the dark sky. I'd always wonder where you'd been. You never told me anything. There's a new guy in town, and he says he loves me, but I don't want to rush things with him. I can't trust anymore, and I don't want to get hurt again. I was broken inside, and he collected all the pieces that you made a mess of. Even though not all the pieces are right, I'm starting to feel whole again. I remember when you were crawling on your knees begging for a second chance. But you didn't say the words I longed for. The mistakes you made were too late to erase. I forgave so many times that I forgot how to anymore. The words you didn't say seemed to float away that cold night. Every time you were out the door, I could feel you slipping away. A part of me that still loves you lingers, hoping you'll come back. It was hard to breathe when you left. You didn't turn back and didn't see me collapse into the ground where you had told me what you did. I forgive you, and I'm just trying to forgive myself. I want to hold you like I did before. I want to feel you smile against my neck and whisper I love you. I want to lay where we lay all those years ago and forget the world. But the part of me that's still holding seems to fade away every day. And I'm starting to let go.

Replacing

Removing you from the system doesn't make me bleed out less
It doesn't make the nights easier to fall asleep
Doesn't even let me breathe with a heavy chest

Subtracting you from the equation doesn't mean there's more room for someone else to fit in
There's still a hole where you left me like a puzzle piece, and I'm incomplete
The air still smells like the remnants of you

Forcing myself to forget we ever had a chance doesn't mean my brain can erase the memories of the moments when time felt like it stopped just for the two of us
It doesn't mean that the boy I fell in love with wasn't ever there at all
It doesn't mean that I don't still want to just hit rewind and go fucking back

Losing you doesn't mean that I don't still feel lost, that I'm not missing a part of me
That I don't still believe I need to right all my wrongs with you, tell you all about my days without you
I still think you care

Folding your note in half, muting your messages, cutting all contact doesn't make you dead in my life
You're still very much alive
And wherever your heartbeat may be, as long as it's beating, mine stays beating too

Simran Kalita

Monday Is Here

It's Sunday.

No, it's Wednesday. Oh, I didn't notice.
Days just pass me by at this point.

It's hard to concentrate when your mind is still clinging.
onto. something. you. never. had.

It's hard to believe, but you best believe it.

Because here I am frozen, time seems to pass me by.
Words that people are telling me turn into echos
That I can't quite make out, stored somewhere else in my
mind.

And for a fleeting moment, I might forget and laugh.
I might even be truly, completely happy for just that
second.
And nothing else could matter, and then the memories seep
in.

And to be honest, I just cringe. I reject my body that felt
those feelings,
said those words to a somebody who turned into a nobody.

I blame myself for being so stupid, but *how could I have
known?*
At least that's what my friends tell me.

And, you know, that's fine. But
What really irks me, shakes me to my core
Is that I mourn the loss of a—I can't get my words around
it—that was never even a—I just don't know the words—to
begin with!

It was something that my voice, my heart, my head
could only wrap around and feel and squeeze but never
really touch.

Because it was never even fucking mine.
It wasn't even anything really. What was it?
How do I explain it?

How do I explain this, what I'm feeling?
Because, technically, it isn't even real, so
How can I feel this way so much?

Now, it's been many Sundays—I think, I'm sure.
And today is Monday. Yes, it is.

Over

After the quiet
There is a storm

After a rainbow
There is a hurricane

After acceptance
There is chaos

After music
There are lyrics to fill the space

After tears
There is a meltdown waiting to happen

After waiting
There is heartbreak

After you
There is moving on

Goodbye my love

It's finally time
I took forever & ages & ages
to finally let you go
You made me whole

Loving you was a part of my daily routine
Just like breathing
But I never knew that I was ready
to be taken off the ventilator

I was so scared to let you go
Grasping, clutching onto a string of balloons
So I could hold onto you
When one by one,
they all flew up above

Your eyes, your smile
Every part about you that invited me in
Just for you to leave again
Disappeared with no goodbye

Your smell, your hair
Your work of art
When you so carefully broke my heart
Even when I happily put it back together
and laid it out in front of you

"Thank god, it's done"
is what all my friends said over and over
But it wasn't ever over
Not for me, it wasn't
Not time and time again

Simran Kalita

Not until you finally pulled out the scissors
Ripped every single string off my back
Holding me down onto the ground
When I fell back into an angel's arms
She carried me back home

It wasn't until I looked in her eyes
That I noticed the mirror she held in front of me
And finally I realized
I was the angel

It's time for my final goodbye
Maybe I'll see you in another life
Maybe one day we'll be one again
But I'm an angel
And this time you'll need to do a lot more
convincing to have me come back down
from heaven

Sometimes I'll sit in the middle of my bed
Wear the blue jacket he wore as a joke one day
Just because I'm missing him

Somedays I'll wake up from a twisted dream
Memories of the night I spent with him
Scrolling back through texts that we poured out to each
other
Not a single person left to tell my secrets to
Staying silent helps me fly higher

You were my comet, my gentle planet
Almost crashed into you, but we passed by just in time
You had to catch your flight, I understand
Loving you makes you less of a man

Sometimes I'll check up on where life takes you
Did you ever find that wonderdust you always dreamed of
Did he ever text me just because?
Did you ever start typing my name just to change your
mind

I miss you
I love you
That's where our story ended
How could you be so cruel
When all I ever did was love you?

Fighting for him
Fighting for the boy who turned my spark into a raging fire
The boy who made me sing in his desire
The boy who made me feel like I was higher
just to be in the same room with you

You will never know the songs I wrote about you
The things I wanted so much to tell you
The voice notes, the paragraphs, the movie scripts,
the photobooth videos, the hour-long rants, the
daydreaming
the everyday yearning,
the calls I almost made
the way you broke my heart in two like it was nothing
When you were everything

All I ever did was love you
All I ever did was love
All I ever did

You didn't deserve an angel
She came down just for you
Now she's flying back above

New Light

The love I had for you
Is seeping from inside of me
Like a poison
I just can't control

It's pouring into a sea of acid
Because it wasn't healthy for me
It took a toll on me
But I am finally being cleansed

Instead, he radiates peace in my life
He spreads my joy
He gives me the strength I need
And that I needed
To get over you

But I can never tell him
I can never cross that line
I can simply wish he sees me one day

Maybe something will be different about me for that
moment
Maybe it's the way I'm wearing my hair
Or how my clothes fit around my bodice
But something will click, and something will change

But until then I can only feel the pressure
Of watching you wash out of me
While he fills me in

Still Not Over You

The other day I was trying to peel a fruit
And my memory flashed back to you

It's been so long
Yet there's a certain feeling I get

When I hear someone say your name

When I remember the things you loved to do so much

When an old joke reminds me of you

I knew you so well
Like the front of my palm, not the back of my hand

I'll hear jokes you share with your friends
And think about how I know everything about that

I creep up on everything you've spent your life doing
And feel like it's part of mine

But today he showed up while I was reminiscing over you
And he was just as much a familiar feeling

And I smiled so hard my face might've cracked open
Because I couldn't concentrate on anything else after that

And suddenly
I'm overthinking everything I say to him
Kinda like how I was for you

But this time it's weird
I think he knows me too
So there's nothing I need to hide
Except for my feelings
I can't do what I did again

Does this mean
Could this mean
I finally love someone else

It's small, fleeting maybe
Temporary and so out of the ordinary
But I think it might be true

I think I am falling for someone else
And I think I'm finally over you.

Restorance

Give me back the days
The days that I spent dreaming with my eyes wide open

Return those nights
The nights I stayed awake hoping to see your comet pass
by

Hand me back my breath
The breath I lost speaking of you to everyone I know, even
if it was only my shadow

Return to me those hours
Spent tirelessly repeating only your name before, after, and
in unison with every thought

Give me back the praise
The praise I sung for you, written in the words of every
song, carved on my hands and in your conscience

Ship me my presence
The being with you no matter how many miles distanced
us, the gift of my love in everything I touched

No need to return my heart
It's ok
I only left a piece of her with you as a token
A lucky charm

But please

Simran Kalita

Send me back my goodness
My kindness, my precious softness
Which I extended to you so naively, unconditionally
And you shattered so easily
Breaking the wings of an angel who tried to rescue you

Your ungrateful sins
Give me back my ease of laughter
The shine in my eyes
The sweetness in my voice
The good in my soul
The light in my smile
Return to me who I was before I suffered a storm like you.

The reflection in your eyes when I stand before them

Reality check

When you're young you think you're invincible
And when that dream shatters
You don't know what to do
With those million pieces of your brain, soul, and heart
That have been splattered into every corner
And you cry and you cry
As though no one has howled before
And that trust that you held close to your heart
Is gone, as if it were stolen
The little wounds that you had sewn up
Open as though they were as fresh as the first hour
Any word that someone says pours salt over your flesh
And you feel like you have nothing left to do
Your rage reminds you of your monsters
Your pain reminds you of your suffering
And you pray for it to stop
But it gets worse and worse until it turns numb
You wonder what it would be like to be dead
Because then maybe the pain would end
And yes, you wouldn't see joy again
But at least, you wouldn't be hurting others or yourself
No person is the solution, no place is a solace
No land offers comfort
No words commence recovery
You lie in a pool of your own filth and blood
And dream of seeing stars because your teary eyes now
block your vision
And you forget that there exists tomorrow
Because nothing can be worse than today
Waves hit you all over again
While you're a statue lost at sea
Unable to move to think to breathe
That's when reality checks in.

know Me

hold Me, throw Me, consume Me, confuse Me, forget Me,
covet Me, scatter Me, surrender Me, arouse Me, denounce
Me, love Me, loathe Me, fire Me, fly with Me,

but don't control Me.

Simran Kalita

My eyes

When you're pouring into me
I wonder if you second a glance
Into my eyes

Do you see your natural reflection in them?
Do you see the way I see you?
Do they mark the silhouette I so carefully draw you with?

While I may not have blue or green orbs
Chocolate like my favorite candy
I contain an ebony so dark it is void of color

So robbed of other hues that their power comes from what
they take in
My eyes are the color of yours when you look into them
They are a mirror to anything and anyone, any place that
passes by

While I see the bountiful world through my own vision
Are you restricted to only see what I see?
I can understand how that's frustrating

I'm sorry you don't have a swimming pool to submerge
yourself in
Or emeralds that shine and stun you at every glance
Or even chestnut that reminds you of home

It took me a long time to fall in love with these eyes
But it helped that my mother always saw a twinkle in them,
stars from the light my eyes captured
And their shape so slanted, I wondered if anyone saw my
soul in them

When you look into my eyes
I hope you see it is only me staring back
I hope that you see my love reflected in them because that
is who I am looking at

Home

Who am I supposed to call
Who am I supposed to talk to now
How can I replace the position you had in my life

Who is going to be there in the same way
Who is going to love me the same way
Who is going to accept me the same way

I didn't ask how you are
Not because I don't care to know how you're doing
But because I can't stand to hear you're doing ok without
me

I wasn't ignoring you
I was doing my best
To pretend I didn't need you the way that I do

After all this
I wonder where the feelings go
Do they disappear or are they on the prowl to capture
someone else

I feel as though I'm a stray dog
My owner left me
Now who do I call home

Waiting and waiting and waiting
And no one is coming to claim me
I'm a gypsy

The Poet Inside Me

Nothing more than a body

Sometimes I stay up at night
And wonder about you and I

Would you love me if I was wrapped in a different body
If my hair was a different color
If my eyes had a brighter glow

Would you choose me if I spoke less
If I stayed quiet when I speak up
If I dreamed about different things

Sometimes I look in the mirror passing by,
or at photos I take of myself
And think about all the possibilities

If my chest weren't fuller
If my spine didn't fold into a curve the way it does at the
bottom
Would people notice me

If I didn't laugh unabashedly
If my voice wasn't this way
If my eyes weren't hiding the many questions behind this
smile

Sometimes I think about the secrets I unlocked for the ones
I've loved,
about the person that's reflected through them
And I wonder if I'm worth it

I walk alone and sit in cars watching traffic rush past
I write poems and dream of things seemingly beyond the
scope of reality
And I tie my love within a box stored deep inside my heart

Simran Kalita

I pick apart the things I do
And why I do them
Who I let into my quiet frantic life

I crave a lot but so little at the same time
I seek chaos but I'm hungry for the day I can be at peace
And I let passersby feel a bit of what I'm feeling when I
open up my heart

There are no secrets left to hide
No mountains I want to climb
No rocks I want to cradle myself under

I feel as though my life could be simplified to a single
poem
Much like this one
No rhyme or repetition
No flow to spiral through, but loaded with metaphors and
analogies and teardrops that land between the stanzas

I'm not sad
I'm just inquisitive

If my mind didn't have these doubts
If my heart was not a fool, easily falling into the hands of
any person, place, or thing that makes it feel special
If my body was not the one I was gifted, that I so carefully
choose to groom

Would I have the same value
Would I attract different looking faces seeking a home
within me
Would I still have the same thoughts

Sometimes I wonder if people would care what I have to
say
If I wasn't pretty

I wonder if the ones I loved so much would love me back
If they saw my soul instead of the shell that confines it

When I look into the mirror, I wonder which part of me I
am staring at
The face I've always had or the one I've always wanted

When I spend a night deep in conversation
Did they think my ideas were brilliant?
Did he like what I had to say
Or is everyone just staring at my tits

Sometimes I wonder
I wonder a lot
If we could separate and reevaluate who we are on the
inside, the filling of our personalities,
Pit against the natural canvas we call our bodies

If I didn't write
If I didn't dream
If I wasn't loud
If I wasn't funny
If I looked different
If I belonged someplace else
Would I still be me
Or would I be much like what I'm worried I appear to be
Would I be nothing more than a body

What was it that you wanted from me—because I gave you everything and now you want nothing?

Weak

Tied by the hands of my own heart
Forced to think that I wasn't in the dark
I feel stupid and used

Telling me what it means to you
What I mean to you
You're just a body

The shame and the guilt and the tears hit me all at once
And there's not a warm bed to crawl into
Escape from my reality

The eyes are on me
The laughter's getting louder
I feel just like wasted plastic

I wish someone had told me
To tread safely
I want to fall asleep

Used and abused
Whispered secrets into my ears
My head knew better, my heart's been M.I.A.

I haven't seen her in a long time
I lost her to someone else too long ago
But as soon as you put your hands all over me, she came
crawling back

I don't owe anything to anyone
But I owe something to myself
But what if the truth is what I owe, and I still don't know
what that is?

Simran Kalita

Still believing in fairytales and made-up stories
Time and time again reality has scoffed in my face
What did I do to deserve this?

I am not a victim
I am tied by the hands of my own heart
Gagged by the jacket of who I love

Praying for someone to be the solace
Something to make this nightmare go away
Everything fades into one big storm

I just want to be saved
I don't think I can do it again
I'm too scared of myself

The scars on my hand prove it
No one asks any questions
I always ask the questions

Giving more than receiving
I'm tired of this charade
Give me the life I crave or death

There's no in-between
There's no escaping
There's no saving me

I'm weak
Too weak
Drowning

Rapture

You with your soulless eyes
Gathering up every square inch of my body
Examining the plot, waiting to pounce
As if I were the reward for your extended starvation

If looks could kill
You'd swallow me alive

You with your devilish smile
Your false pretenses and jovial voice
You feed on the territory you are given
And still ask for more

If the Pied Piper existed
You'd be the slaughterhouse the children were taken to

You with your sinister heart
You put your hands where they don't belong
And replace with tears every block of skin
Generations of rage will find you in hell

If I could kill
I'd tie you to a rock at the bottom of the sea

Simran Kalita

Gardener

I bloom like a delicate flower into your arms
And what do you do?
You tear me from my roots
Wrong me from my very core

Making your way through my petals
Up to my long stem,
A solid backbone
But which bended easily for you

And you kissed me right at the start of my bud
And played with my fruits
Promised me the day and the night
But forgot how to water me

Forgot what I needed and what I deserved
You forgot to water the elephants and the lions and tigers
In your wonderful garden
And worst of all, I fret
You forgot to water your plants

My, what a man like you can do standing there
What with your bold stature and humble voice
Almost had me disbelieving all I have seen!
But I won't fall for your reckless abandonment of the green
thumb

For I am going somewhere,
somewhere far from you
Somewhere deep in a forest or near a cottage or a farm
But as far away as I can get
To a dear one's house who will water me everyday

And in the end

And in the end, it wasn't me. It isn't me that you're going to choose. It isn't me that you'll wake up next to in the morning. It isn't me who gets anything more than the flowers you got me, the notes you sent me, the gifts and compliments you showered me with. In the end, it was all meant for someone else. Such is my curse. To be desired but never loved. To be wanted but never had. I have been blessed with the most beautiful things in life, but what point is that of beauty when it is never cherished? I rot as the flowers rot and the untouched food rots and the things you said that made me feel rot. Your hands, they touched a part of my soul that no one else knows. Your eyes looked into mine like they had never seen light before. Your voice washes over me as though no other sound exists. My poetry exists because of you. My songs exist because you exist. My lyrics hold meaning because you stumbled into my life. My music is true because you are here. My tears run long because it's you behind them. My wounds cut deep because you are the one who holds the knife. No one seems to do anything the way that you do. And with your magical gaze and enchanting sweet nothings, you carefully blinded me with a cloth. You made me feel. You made me think. You made me stumble again. Why throw rocks at my window if you have no intention of coming up? Why say things that make me fantasize you and I in my head? You're so cruel and selfish, and the only person you hurt is yourself. You're hurting me now because of you. I have no more love to give, no more tears to cry. When all the world's supplies run out, I have no more left than I did before. I have nothing, and it's you who's taken everything. Are you happy now?

Why so faithful

How faithful are these eyes
That bury every tear inside like a prison
How faithful are these hands
That shudder even at my own touch
How faithful are my dreams
That know you belong to someone else and have been
vacant ever since

Disclaimer

Contrary to popular belief
My poems are not about people
My poems are about feelings
The memories, the capsules I store them inside

My poems are about how much, how deep my capacity to
feel can penetrate
They are about the joys and sadness that spur from an
action or event
They are about the things that make me weak, made me
revel in my thoughts
They are about the ways I have been moved

Because contrary to my own belief
My poems cannot be about a person
They cannot resurrect the one I have so carefully described
in every letter of every word, wrapped in gold and silver
along with my heart's pieces
They cannot bring to life what was only enclosed within the
two dimensions of my notebook paper

No matter how much I try
The person whom I thought was so possibly real
Simply does not exist beyond the scope of this book
They surely cannot live in a reality where there is a them
without me

My poems cannot describe real people
For they put to test the godliness of those who are barely
capable in the real world
They make it seem as though the ones I love are carved by
Michelangelo himself
That they aren't just a nobody seeking a place in a life
where the only one who recognizes them to be a somebody
is me

These poems are not a falsity
They are very real indeed
But they are true to me, in the words I retell to my friends
after a night of being whisked away, in the things I describe
with so limited a vocabulary
They are true to me but only me

My poems are not about people
They simply can't be if those people leave
If those people hurt me, if those people burn me
Because now why would I write poems about somebody
who would so easily refuse me

Pretty Eyes

Today a woman told me I have pretty eyes, but I didn't believe her because you never lost yourself in them like I did in yours.

Perfect Broken Doll

You picked your favorite doll
From the glass window of the most coveted toy shop
Where you spent countless hours pressing your cheeks
against the window
Hoping, praying. one day

And she was perfect right back
Your little trinket
You carried her around in your pocket
Dressed her up, flew her around your room

Till one day you had the puppeteer tie strings around her
back
So you wouldn't lose her
So she couldn't run away

And you still dressed her up,
Still threw her around your room

You bought her the prettiest things:
A doll house made of gold,
A closet filled with diamonds & tiaras

And all she did
Was wait for you
She dreamed of dancing in the moonlight
Bathing in the river
Holding your hand so she knew her way home

But you locked a songbird in a cage
Trapped her in oh-so-sweet honey
Told her it was her own fate
And threw away the key

Now you're older, gray hairs cover your skin like a forest
And the twinkle of childhood in your eyes
Has turned into but a glimmer of the force you used to be

And your precious doll is all tattered up
Unfolding and breaking at the seams
She is but a shell of the toy you picked up that day.

She died one day,
Silently surrounded by jewels & inanimate, invaluable
objects
Because you never noticed her,
Never let her dance,
Never let her leave

Her castle walls crumbled around her,
though her doll house was intact

You never even noticed her
The life that zoomed out of her
The laughter she used to spread
The kindness she would radiate
The talent that came with ease

And she fell apart, but she is still your perfect broken doll
Because you would rather own a broken doll
Than one that was free

Writer's block

I'm in need of inspiration
Without you, there are no profound thoughts
No actions, no final stands
No tides, no sun to welcome the day

Your memories reach a part of me that know no ulterior
desire
How can you be so perfect
When you are so imperfectly downfallen in everyone's
eyes
The truth is
Half of you is your every good deed, your every winning
smile
The hand that held my heart
The other half is my dreams that kept you alive

How can we be so perfect
Yet never see the light of another day
Maybe we aren't what we seem
If only you saw the parts of me other than what I let you
see
The flood of hunger at the mention of your name
The rush of adventure to be by your side

How can you not love me
When I was sent to you to be plucked
When I was delivered to heal
Designed to carry the wings that would crush anyone that
would hurt you
To put to sleep your nightmares
And stay awake to hear your stories

On any day, your voice can guide me out of my own dark
forest
Days like today, I wish we could remember what it felt like
To hold each other closer than possible
Nights like this, I miss you dearly

My heart won't stop calling out for you
It doesn't know any better,
For it has never loved before
And it is worried there will never be a love quite like this
after

I know we're not meant to be
But if you hold me for just one night,
Could we pretend we are for just that one night?

I'm in need of inspiration
And a single gaze into your eyes
Could capture mine for long enough
I'll know exactly what to say
And you'll allow yourself to stay
So that I can finish this one thought
Instead of thinking of everything
Only to say nothing

Poetry (part two)

Writing love notes to someone who doesn't read them
Painting pictures for someone who's blind
Pouring more and more out of myself in exchange for
pieces of you

Lying under the stars hoping to catch a glimpse of your
comet
Slipping deeper and deeper into an ocean of translucent
creatures
I'm your only addiction

I'm the bad habit
I'm your muse, the only picture your camera captures
I'm the drunk haze that makes you smile when you're
wasted
I'm the pair of eyes that shines just for you

You can capture me and hide me in your caged heart
Drink a little more of me every time
Graze over my skin with your smooth fingers
Hold me tight as I collapse within myself, I'm breaking
apart
Claim me, finally

Finishing

And at the end of the tunnel, I knew I had to jump out of the car, with no brakes, nobody driving anymore, heading towards flames and a big wall. I fell into the bushes, got up, wounded, and walked past him. He was the driver, but I was guiding him along the way. I guess at some point, enough was enough, and he wanted to call out. So I gathered the broken pieces of myself around me, told my heart any excuse to get over him, and worked on myself. Every fucking day I woke up having slept only three hours. I couldn't help that I stayed up for hours forgetting about work, listening to music, and watching the night sky say goodbye. I tried to distract myself with people, faces when I saw him in every crowd I passed by and looked around for him at every corner I turned, every room I entered. I let everybody invalidate my feelings while I let the wind blow coldness into my face and pretended to smile at their stories. Every day I built myself up back again, brick by brick. Applied makeup to hide the dark crevices on my face where you could see what he left behind, posted as if I was fine and happy again, and convinced myself I was ok. I wanted to prove myself in this lonely world, where all I wanted was for someone to worry I got home ok, ask me what my favorite things were. I wanted all the prettiest things to surround me, wanted to be the most beautiful girl he ever lost, but it didn't matter at the end. And somewhere, I think, trying and pretending to be ok, I learned how to actually be ok. Though I fed myself excuses for why it didn't work out and why I'm better off without him, it didn't really matter at the end. Because I was whole again, without him, regardless of the why's and the but's. But then why am I here again, staring at my reflection of the girl who was so in love with a boy who only hurt her, when I want to love someone else. It just doesn't make sense, but maybe I need to work more and try again, because maybe I have not yet healed completely. Yes, my wings are sewn back together, but I have not learned to fly again. I might keep pretending, the same way I got myself around last time, I'll do it again. Maybe it's time or maturity, but I need a bit of both to get me through the aftershocks of you.

The Poet Inside Me

Needed to find myself before I could lose myself with you

Patience

I waited for tears to take it away
I waited for pain to take it away
I waited for years passing by to take it away
I waited for the distance to take it away
I waited for the last conversation to take it away
I waited for someone else to take it away
I waited for her hands on you to take it away
I waited for forgiveness to take it away
I waited for months of therapy to take it away
I waited for the loud nights and blurry mornings to take it
away
I waited for the alcohol to take it away
I waited for the drugs to take it away
I waited for my parents to take it away
I waited for their love to take it away
I waited for the last memories of our wordless fight to take
it away
I waited for the time you took to come home to take it away
I waited for the lies, the false promises to take it away
I waited for you to take it away
I waited for joy to take it away
I waited for friends to take it away
I waited for the emptiness to take it away
I waited for the loneliness to take it away
I waited for the acts committed to forego my loneliness to
take it away
I waited for the unhappiness to take it away
I waited for the cut and the blood to take it away
I waited for your kisses to take it away
I waited for your hands to take it away
I waited for the spark, the lying with someone else to take it
away
I waited for my strength to take it away
I waited for every day to take it away

I waited for sleep to take it away
I waited for the sleeplessness to take it away
I waited for the anger to take it away
I waited for my denial to take it away
I waited for the realization that this could never work, that I
am broken way beyond repair, to take it away
I waited for the wind to take it away
I waited for the warm sun to take it away
I waited for snow to take it away
I waited for the rain after a drought to take it away
I waited for home to take it away
I waited for love to take it away
I waited for hate to take it away
I waited for what seemed like forever to take it away
I waited for wings to sprout out behind me to take it away
I waited for the endless fighting with myself and others to
take it away
I waited for my broken heart to be patched up to take it
away
I waited until I realized there's no taking it away
And now I wait every day.

You're a temporary solution to the madness that grows
inside of me.

Her

Really dropped the diamond ring, huh
Really decided not to walk out through the door

Does she listen to you talk for hours
Does she listen
Does she listen to the things you say
Does she care
Does she tell you about your flaws, your potential, your
super powers
Does she

Does she think about you all the time
Does she stay
Does she cry when you don't call her
Does she
Does she wait for you to reply
Does she lose herself in her thoughts about you
Does she give up herself just to dream about being in your
arms
Does she

Let me love somebody else
Let me love someone else
Let me love anyone else

I'm not religious, but for you—
You've got me praying to god I love someone else

Did she imagine the late night drives
Did she imagine you'd be there at the airport
Did she call
Did she imagine you'd call
Did she wait for you to call
Did she think you'd drive her places
Did she want to go home with you
Did she
Did she do the same things I did for you

You've got me feeling like a pillowcase
I'm mad replaceable, wasted space
You don't really even need me
When all you do is sleep in the comfort of others, other
things, other places
Other faces

Did she imagine the life you guys would have
Was she that fucking stupid
Was she that pathetic
Was she
Did she fall in love with you
Did she always forgive you
Did she

I want to know because I did all these things, I fucking did
I really really did every single one of them, why oh why
did I do them

Did she play you every single one of her songs
Did she tell all her friends she's in love with you, that
you're the one
Did she
Will she live with the regret her whole life, knowing Prince
Charming didn't even want Cinderella

Cinderella's crying all the time now
She's in her castle, but she's crying
She's in the sun, but she's crying
She's at the beach, but she's crying
She's stealing somebody's kisses, but she's crying
Cinderella's breaking others' hearts now, leaving a trail of
them on her way to her dungeon
Where she sits and cries all fucking day

She just wants a break

Was she your Cinderella?
Was she
Was she the exact blonde hair, blue eyes you wanted

Forfeit the things you said, take back the words you
dropped in my hands
Turn the music off, because it's glaringly loud
I'm losing my mind, can't you tell

I'm so overwhelmed
Forgetting the pain and the agony every time you come
around
They can't say I haven't loved
But I feel so stupid
I'm so fucking loser

How could I
Could she
Could she feel this way about you
Could she let it get this far
Could she let it slip into an ocean with you, let you play her
around and dance as long as you're with her
I could

And I want to stop, so fucking bad
Take me back
Take me back to the moment
Not the one where you were with me, so close
Not where we stood next to each other
Not where you ran after me
Not where you walked next to me
Not where you couldn't take your eyes off me
Not where you couldn't stop talking about me
Not where you couldn't get enough of me
Not where you realized you loved me
Not where you didn't want to leave me
Back to where we first met
In the courtyard, right before 2
I wish I'd never met you
Erase me, oh mine

Let the memories of you fade away
Let me forget all the love
Let me remember only the heartbreak
Let me climb up that tall ass mountain
Let me breathe fuller
Let me love myself
Let me love someone else
Let me love again

For without you, I'm no one
I'm half the person I ever was
I'm not the person I thought I was
I'm not the person I ever was
I'm never going to be whole again

Does she
Does she feel that way about you
She could never

I'm Sorry

I'm sorry I didn't text back
I'm sorry I never let you know I was back in town
I'm sorry I left all your messages on delivered
I'm sorry I never bothered to reply

I know so much time has passed
I'm sure I'm barely a stolen nothing to you now
But I do think about you
And how I hurt you

When you must have been pacing,
waiting for me to respond
It won't make you feel better,
but there's a string of broken hearts
that trail behind me

Pieces and people I let crumble
waiting for that one guy to text me back
And only now that it's much too late
Do I realize all the things you could've given me

And it's not to say that I want them now
But maybe if things were different,
you could've gotten back more than what you gave
But you deserve someone who cherishes you
the way you cherished me

And I deserve someone who cherishes me
the way I cherished him

Simran Kalita

I let you fill the emptiness, the void
he left behind
Let you make me feel the part of him
that I was always craving
Ran my hands through your hair
The way I always wished I did with him

I let you kiss my lips that were sealed
just for him
I let you touch parts of me
that meant more than just my body
Even though I had kept them safely
for the man I actually loved

I let you feel like you had made a difference,
like you meant something deeper
When your hands went deeper
And reached a certain part of my soul
but not in a good way
Because I decided to give those things away

I let my hands travel to give you pleasure
Let my fingers caress your head & heart
I unfolded the buds I clutched so quietly,
only to feel so empty when it became dark

I let you put your mouth on me
And kiss different parts of me
I invited you in with my soul-filled eyes
I let you believe
that this night was all that you'd need
I let you in with a ticket
for a movie you couldn't even imagine
in your wildest fantasies

I'm sorry that I let myself imagine
Your gentle curls might have had
the same texture as his
I'm sorry that I imagined kissing him
when I was yours for that night

I'm sorry that I let you hold me so tight
I'm sorry your arms were around me
Your touch aroused me
But only because I pictured it was him

I'm sorry, you don't deserve that
Your world means so much more
Than that night when I promised you so much
Please don't feel like I used you

I let you fill in the parts of me
Where I only wanted his body
I let myself believe this was okay
That this was what everyone does these days
But I'm not doing ok

I'm sorry because you deserve a thousand apologies
And so do all the others,
whose hearts I played with recklessly
When all along my own heart was simply a toy
In the man I love's world

I'm sorry that my charm, my body
Let you believe I needed you urgently
I'm sorry the choices I made
Let you slowly slip into
my home, my hands, in me
I'm sorry that you wanted me

Simran Kalita

I'm sorry because that isn't an excuse
But something that is so broken
Can't be expected to fix the things around it
I'm sorry that when your love should've molded me
Instead it only reminded me
that I wasn't good enough

I'm sorry that despite your kind eyes, your sweet smile
Your laughter, the way you talked
The things we talked about
Nothing you could say could ever be enough
To pull me away

I'm sorry that I let you imagine a reality
Where I was always found underneath your sheets
That I might bring you home with me
That you might find the one you've been looking for
in me

I'm sorry because I shouldn't have stabbed you with a
thousand knives
Just because I found a dagger in my back
I'm sorry that words can't express how sorry I am
I'm sorry that I can't help but still regret that night
I'm sorry that a sweet memory remains as trauma with me
I'm sorry that I didn't say no and let you try to love me
I'm sorry that you thought things would be easy with me

I'm sorry I let you believe you were the man for me
I'm sorry that no words, no body could ever compete

I'm sorry that I am so incomplete

without him.

The Poet Inside Me

Loyalty eats me

Forget what you said
Forget what we meant

Imagine me falling onto the covers
Right where you laid

Holding him to pull him closer to me
Fading when the regret hits me in the head

His smell lingers on every part of me that it sticks to
From the taste of his lips to his hair on my chest

None of it was you
Wishing it was you

Smelling him on me where you were supposed to be
Thinking of the moment I knew it was over

Thinking of the way he touched me
Exactly where you were supposed to

The way I combed his hair with my fingers
The way I meant to do sitting next to you

The dream collapses into my reality
Because it's not you, it's him.

Heartburn

You've made your decision
Keep me locked out as far away as possible
No persuasion
Can't convince the blind to open their eyes

But tell me why it still burns
The curves of your face under my hands
Am I still praying
Look up to a sky with no color

Forever spiraling
Second-guessing
Do you think you're the only one?
Because you are

Watch my moves
As you burn me with every touch
Motion palms beat
Target the weak

A quiet rhythm
Building up
Fire eyes
Caught in your desert storm

Perfect match
Competition too strayed
Wild racing
Fighting against you, fighting for you

Make the pain stop
Erase the wounds you left me with
Compress this broken heart
She's refusing to beat again

Why does it feel this way?
Keep me as your prisoner
Your cuffs tethered to my throat
Or set me free

Simran Kalita

Extreme perfectionism

Nothing is ever enough
Not this piece of art, nor the way that you look at me
It's like you don't even need me
I'm using every inch of my fingers to mold the shape of
clay
That lies across the table from you
Pushing and pulling and over-perfecting
Because it's still not good enough
Light foundation on every inch of my skin because my
reflection isn't perfection
Doing and redoing and throwing it all out again
Dyeing the colors that take you back to harmony
Chewing on chalk to make my voice sound like a
symphony
Molding and folding till my fingers go numb and fall off
steadily
It's like you can't even see me
I have a case of extreme perfectionism
One that makes everyone hate me
However the antidote is your company
I'm worried even that won't get it rid from me

Saans (Translated: Breath)

Breathing is simple
It's as easy as breathing
they say

I wish I could just breathe
Instead of struggling every moment
I wish I didn't think life was slipping out of me
every time I took one step in the wrong direction

To not be able to do this most basic thing
Am I broken
It should be so simple

But I feel so broken
Every breath feels like a tornado
That's about to hit
And I'm simply lying awake in the eye

I feel so broken
My back hurts
My lungs hurt
My head hurts
My heart hurts

I'm losing myself
Holding on
To any piece I have left
Shaken from the trauma
Every time I can't breathe again

Time

We never stop to think
Of what could have
Been

We never stop to wander
To touch
To smile
To caress

We revolve in this
Revolution

We are dissolved in the
Illusion

Of what we call home
Love, planet

Laughter is the absence
Of mind

Eyes reach deep into the
Pockets of our souls
And deceive us
In this world of
Blooming

I am swallowed from
underneath.

Water

I feel so empty in my stomach
With nothing inside me

I miss the fountain
That washes over me
Warming every inch of my skin

I miss the river
That swims right through me
Unfolding every flower

I feel so full in my thoughts
Consumed by words and expressions

I miss the lighthearted laughs
The days where only sun
Could touch me with happiness

I feel so drowned in this sea of hatred
With the waves towering over me
Washing me in their dark blue
Endlessness

The winds that graze my face
The flowers that graze my fingers
The mind that was so free

I feel so hollow on this planet
With the Mother Earth
Sitting beside me

What'll Take It

This is where it ends

This is where the road starts to get smaller

This is where people look at me differently

This is where dreams become a scarcity

This is where love is thrown into oblivion

This is where a pool of you and I are scattered

This is where hearts are tossed when we're finished

This is where the mind gives up and beats you down

This is where smiles turn sickly as you stare longer

This is where hands get rough and arms get hairy

This is where it all ends

This is where it begins.

(This is where we start to heal.)

The Poet Inside Me

Finally

I spent so long thinking about you
I forgot about myself
I spent so long dreaming about you
My inner fantasies fell asleep

Climbing the vines that trapped me so long ago
Finally found a way out
Even though you're not coming with me
I felt like I left you to suffer

Choices, choices so many I have to live with
But choosing to love you is not a regret
Choosing to stay started to sound like one
Now I hope leaving won't make any more

Finally breathing the way I never thought I could
Letting the air whisper out my every unuttered thought
Letting your hands unfold every flower I kept from
blossoming
You used me as your vessel

Feeling empty but so numb
Seeing war with no memories
Trauma I suppressed with every smile of yours
Now I'm flying

I want to see what it's like
To feel butterflies with another
Lock eyes with another
Talk endlessly, feel comfort with another

Simran Kalita

You gave me all you could
But that wasn't enough
Especially when you gave yourself not an ounce of that
And didn't let me help

I could make you a list
Convincing you of our unwritten story
But that would be pointless
When you're miles away staring out your window

I could scream from the rooftops
But what's the point if you're deaf
I could paint you a thousand portraits
But your tears have made you blind

There's no regret
There's nothing I could do
So I choose to float away
Riding on the back of another

I hope you find love
I hope you find me again
I hope you remember
I hope you remember yourself

I'm always here
But I'm finally starting to love myself
When for so long
I only remembered you

Anachrysm

(noun)
The art of faking it till you make it

Fire

Pick a fire

Watch it burn

Let it scorch you from the inside

It can't touch you on the outside

You're lost, aren't you?

You're a lost soul

You've traveled miles and miles in a circle

But you didn't know it

Learned to fend for yourself in this jungle safari named life

Where people's words stung more
Than a lion's growl

Where people's unspoken biases pinched more
Than a tiger's bite

You've been at it for so long
Why don't you take some rest?

You've been fighting a one-manned side of a deadly war

And you never even took a breath

Calm down, wait here
I'll bring you some water

The Poet Inside Me

You can water your beloved plants and animals

You can choose now where you want to travel

There is a choice: and you can choose yourself

No one will blame you, for no one even knows you here
So, what does it matter?

Let the fire subside beside you

Let yourself be engulfed in it, divulge in it
Spread yourself in it

You couldn't spread your clipped angel wings before,
when it would've made sense
when a thousand eyes kept you from doing so

But you can now, here floating in this fire
You can choose to spread your wings

They are no longer clipped, that part of you was washed
away
From either the flames you ride in or the water you glide in

So spread your wings and allow them to take you high
above the sky
They now have fiery tips,
an anger, a rage, which is all-consuming but all-needed

You are now yourself, your own person

Because it didn't take a relentless circle of battles

It only took a single fire.

Beautiful dolls

Oh little girl
Why do you crave being like those other girls
The ones with pink ribbons in their hair
And sparkles on every dress they wear

Oh little girl
Why can't you see
That your braided hair and Walmart clothes
Have a tale to tell that no one knows

The wrinkles on your father's shirt
Are ironed straight the moment he comes home
The loneliness in your mother's eyes
She sees you, and somehow, that also hides

You're standing on the very ground
That your parents fought to be recognized on
The sense of pride in their country's eyes
Can never be equivalent to the judgy looks of those
passersby

I know the world has tugged you along
And you're much too young to understand
Your innocence flutters in those wondering eyes
Why don't they like me no matter how hard I try?

Oh little girl
You're much too precious for this surface world
Where your thoughts will one day make you inestimable
And those that gather around you will lift you rather than
point at you

Until then remember the feeling of home
In your mother's chest you're snuggled into when morning
wakes you
The pitter patter of your baby brother's feet as he races
through the narrow halls
The toys you brought with you from your old town

And when you are older, I hope you never forget
Your bangles hold the weight of your culture's depth
Your kajal drawn at the rims of your eyes
Wraps you in the protection of those generations who have
lived so that you could survive

You may be lured into buying pretty things
But remember who your parents have raised within
The stories of their parents that guide you till this day
Are the blueprint of the person who will make their way

Oh little girl
Though they will not say it
Your parents do love you more than words can express
They love you so much they will buy you every sparkly
dress

Do not compare your worth to that of others
For life will teach you what matters most is above us
Your feet should stay planted firmly on the ground
While your dreams can soar to limits profound

Oh little girl
You beautiful thing
The way you look takes my breath away
No need to wish god had made you any other way

Your life is a gift
Your brain so sound
To understand and create a home with everything
happening all around
You are the very essence of how beautiful dolls are made

(There comes a time in every immigrant daughter's life
where she questions her identity. There is no stopping this
feeling from arising—her life's events, family, and
quizzical nature have brought her to this moment, but in
time, she will finally see that she is exactly how she's
meant to be.)

Greedy

I always wanted the best things in life to surround me
I wouldn't settle for less
I thought it stemmed from something inside me
That never received the love it needed from people,
so it resorted to gaining that attention from things.

I had plans, goals, and everything was motivated by
Material possessions.
Because I wanted to seem accomplished, like an equal
Among others.
But even if I worked so hard, earned all that money,
and truly did earn the right to be an equal,
What would it amount to?

The right to flaunt a life of artificial luxury?
An adoring jealousy in friends?
A disapproving comment from outsiders?

I would still not win.

There is nothing in this world that can replace
What I have lost inside on the outside.
There is no necklace, no purse that I wouldn't give up
For one more hour laughing under the sun with my friends.
No amount of numbers on cheques or karats on diamonds
Would be enough to steal me from a night with my puppy
Following me around everywhere.

I don't need those things, don't want those things anymore.
I reject their standings, rob them of their power and hold
over me.

I used to think that if I had all those possessions to decorate
me
I'd appear more beautiful, more desirable and coveted
But now that I have lived the life I have with open eyes,
I realize that no matter how beautiful I am, those who
Hurt me will still do their damage.
In fact, I'd be more of a porcelain doll with a higher
pedestal
To be thrown off of.

She didn't care
That she thought I was the most beautiful girl she had ever
seen.
She didn't care
That I bared my heart to her and cried over him.
She did what she needed to and left the scraps for me to
pick up.

After so much sweat, I realized that what I thought I
wanted to be
Was a fragmented reflection of the person I thought I was.

I thought I was being goal-minded, self-motivated,
Unperturbed by others because I had me and with that,
came
Along all the worldly treasures & pleasures I seek.

But no fancy words or airs could change the fact that I was
simply
Greedy.

The other woman

I don't want to be the other woman
I refuse to be that girl
I can't be your dirty little secret
I can't be the one you pine over
I won't be the one you pine over

I refuse to be the fantasy that you sleep soundly dreaming
about
The same that keeps her awake at night
I refuse to enable her to live a life trying to fill any inch of
my shadow
Comparing her every move to the way I dance in your head
The same that you thirst over when the memory of me
revisits you

I refuse to be the wild-eyed comrade
The one you came so close to but never captured
I don't want to be disrespectful
But for both parties involved it's best we leave things as is
I'm not the one you're supposed to think was the one

I refuse to let myself be a part of any dream world other
than that of the man I marry
He's the only one I want
The only one I want to want me
Others came close but you almost won
That thought makes everything feel scary

I don't want to be the other woman
I don't want to be the dream girl
I hate to see the things it does to you, worse for the things it
does to her
I reject the labels that the crowds, her friends, your friends
would eventually throw at me, without even knowing me

Simran Kalita

I'm not the other woman, and because I'm a woman, I will
do everything in my power to make sure I won't be

God if society would let me, I'd move to an island and live
off berries and being barefoot
And I'd only let women come near me

Simran Kalita

What Makes A Woman

What makes a woman
Is her ability to be anything

She can be tough
She can be soft

She can be simple
She can be poised
She can be rigid
She can be firm

But she is not moldable
She is not foldable
She cannot dissolve
In your hands

What breeds a woman
Is her complex design
Within

She can be thoughtful
She can be rash
She can be timid
She can have rage

What shapes a woman
Is her bounty of space
She can be tiny
She can be tall
She can be skinny
She can have curves

What defines a woman
Is her very essence
She blooms a flower in
The Center of her
Existence

She can give life
She can live life
She can change life
And she can choose life

What makes a woman
Is her ability to choose
To be who she wants
To have what she wants
To live how she wants
And To love Herself the
Way She wants.

Simran Kalita

An exquisite garden

Do not compare a rose to a tree
You might think it's strange
But have you ever wished so hard to be a rose when your
trunk was as long as one could grow

The tree is everlasting
Its roots so grounded
Every branch is an ornament
With multicolor leaves sprouting throughout
Sometimes its fruits bared are raved about

While a rose is a classic
Its beauty in its deep scarlet petals
Overlapping to create an unheard-of texture
With thorns prickled through to warn others
And a fragrance so lovely one must remember

No matter how hard a rose tries
It can never be the wise, looming tree
And no matter how much the tree wishes
It will never be the delicate rose

But the two are beautiful
And can grow in a garden beside each other
One sits under a tree reminiscing and pondering
While one plucks a pretty rose to play within one's fingers

This garden may have bunnies and singing birds
Carnations, wild hydrangeas, and bushes shaped in funny
curves
The daytime brings the brilliant sun
While the moon and stars arrive at night

Each creature, each creation so unique
Incomparable to the others
And each growing vibrantly by the creek

One wants one of everything in their beautiful garden
Every element has a part to play
Containing a rhythm as the wind makes everyone sway

Never compare two souls pitted against one another
When they are meant to thrive under the same clouds
down-pouring love

I hope you hope to grow an exquisite garden
Where all the world's beauties know they are all worth a
show

(You're not supposed to be envious of another woman.
You're supposed to admire her beauty, the same way others
admire yours. You have been put on this earth exactly as
you are meant to be; there is no need to alter what someone
so carefully took time into creating. You were meant to
be—the force that you are.

It is society that is responsible for creating competition
between women so beautiful and each deserving of
appreciation. Do not let this silent killer get to you. It has
led many wonderful people astray into making detrimental
decisions to both themselves and others.

And if a man ever makes you feel that you need to compete
with a woman, know that that man is nothing but a blind
fool who is greedy and only knows how to destroy
protected gardens. We let blind fools walk into the thorn
bush. If a woman makes you feel you need to compete with
her, forgive her and walk away. She will learn in time with
your lesson how beautiful you are.)

Maybe this is my story, but maybe this story wrote me.

Runaway

I imagine people walk through these streets
And ask themselves what they are running towards
Or from

I imagine a million fireflies lighting up the sky
Just to lose their spark
When the evening's over

I imagine you slipping under the covers next to me
And I imagine us painting the ceiling & the walls in a
funny color

I imagine the people we walk by have a lot on their mind
Or else they would stop to wait with me

A million voices in my head
A thousand notes in my diary
But only one voicemail from you

I packed my luggage this morning
Took off to the airport
Fastened myself into a future of pining after you

But it was then that I realized I was never more alive
A runaway, hungry for any excuse to get away from
This town, this city, this world

You saved me
Don't take all the credit
I'll see you on the other side of this tunnel
Maybe someday

Simran Kalita

We can finally stop holding on
Keep our love from spilling onto the pages
Of a book we're scared to write our stories in

Let me start.

Thoughts that don't compare

Silent

It's funny
The way that you had a hold over me
The way your every movement, every word had a
gravitational pull on my body, my actions, my thoughts
It's funny the way you never knew

To dream of jumping into you, a free fall I wasn't afraid of
Shut my eyes and prepare for landing
Hoping you catch me at the bottom

Letting the wind sweep my hair all around me, watching
the breeze push our bodies closer
Listening to the world around us but forgetting it at the
same time

Holding onto the moments that made me feel like this was
something
Making sense of things with no point in making sense of
Letting it all be swept under a rug, only to be peeked back
at in the hardest of times

Drawing a castle with you as my emperor, picturing our
hands holding as the flashing lights blind us
You were my everything and nothing at the same time

Grasping onto the reality of those moments, asking
questions that will never get answered, losing my mind
over them

Everyone told me I was wrong, but I still held a candle for
you, I still believed in you! I still loved you

Now I wave a white flag but I have no ill feelings,
admitting my defeat to a bitter no one

The innocent curiosity turned into a point of realization turned into a silent love turned into a silent burn turned into a glimmer of hope turned into a shower of hope turned into a measly list of excuses thrown back in my face turned into my own excuses turned into denial turned into my loss of faith turned into my clutch for love turned into my loss of love.

Your calm ocean no longer causes waves to crash onto my beach.

Your pouring of emotions no longer makes me want to run to you.

At first, I used to not want to like you.
Then, I didn't want to not like you.
Then, I didn't want to want to not like you.
Now, I don't care.

I think that's worse than not liking you.
Let's replace like with love because my blood runs deeper than our bones.

Every time I tried to forget, my brain put together fuzzy pieces of the image of two bunnies fighting with each other, finding each other, making love to each other. And that memory caused a burning sensation at the core of my tummy.

I no longer feel anything. They were simply two animals. We were two humans. We happened to catch their souls interact. So what?

I don't want to know about your thoughts and feelings, and at this point, I don't want to tell you mine either. I am just tired and done with this constant battle, this back and forth, this will she won't she, this fight with myself against my own feelings and against my better judgement.

I wanted to prove them wrong, but I have somehow found a silver lining. And I know no matter what, I come out of this unscathed.

You know what, I don't even want to be your friend—because what is the point of being friends with someone you're in love with. You can't have them, you can't want them, you can't love them. Yet you choose to stay.

I choose myself. I want to be free, free from the shackles of your messy love. Free as a bird flying high above this raging sea.

Please don't make this harder than it needs to be. Please don't make any sense of the things I've done, the things I've said. Let me leave peacefully, and I'll remain a distant acquaintance.

You know, you know all these little things about me. And I know all your intimate details. Please forget them, forget me. Forget what you heard, what you saw, what I told you, what I gave you, what we did, all our memories. Please forget me. Those memories only exist if we let them. They only have meaning if we choose to give that to them. Else they will run along capturing some other unlucky soul. I want to be free.

The thoughts I had about you before make me sick to my stomach now. All that I did to keep you to stay, to keep you here, talking to me. I was pathetic and losing pieces of myself day by day.

Maybe there was a point where we met at the middle, maybe there were several points, but to go through this heartache in all the other moments is not fair to either of us, especially to me.

I won't come to visit, I won't come at all. You won't see me, you won't get near me. Please stay away. As far as you can. Backs pressed against the other side of the wall. Not a limb you can stretch out to reach me.

I have boarded up all the cardboard to protect me in my castle walls—I am sick and tired and sick and tired of you not being there when I am sick and tired. Have some respect. Gather me in bundles please if you can on your side. Send them back to their sender, let me be whole again.

If you choose to stay silent now, stay silent forever.

365

When the world falls quiet
And the fireworks light up the sky
Let the earth beneath you
Swallow you whole without a sound

Give in to the melody
As the music vibrates your body
Let the ringing of their screams
Encapsulate your inner thoughts

Not a soul in the world
Can feel the way you feel
So beautiful, in your bountiful
Arise with the ocean waves

Another revolution around the sun
An inevitable rotation that can't be undone
Kiss the people you want to see again
Kiss me quick, before the year comes to an end

The Poet Inside Me

Stop

Lies lies

Lines lines

Lies Lies

Lines Lines

Lies Lies

Lines Lines

These lies
That drew
The lines

Between us

They carved our souls
Into hollow shapes of
Empty
Air

Lies lies

Lines lines

Lines lies lines lies lines

Lies lines lies lines lies

Lies

Stop.

Simran Kalita

What He Sees

She doesn't look at me the same way
She doesn't smile for me the way
she always used to
I can't find the twinkle in her eyes

It's dead in her eyes
She doesn't move towards me anymore
She doesn't even give me a second glance
Maybe she doesn't feel the same way anymore

Maybe she moved on
Maybe she finally found someone who can
love her the way I never could
Maybe she found someone like I told her to
who holds her the way I only wish I could

Maybe I'm just a friend again
Maybe things really did end
Maybe that night was just a coincidence
And she only took me in
because I'm her closest friend

Maybe it doesn't matter that we slept in the same bed
Maybe she does that often
Maybe I'm not the first guy on the other side
Maybe I should've given that other girl a ride

The Poet Inside Me

I missed the chance when I could've
had the most beautiful thing right in my arms
Maybe I'm not making sense
Clearly her love wasn't as intense
to keep you up at night
Trying to call her even if it's just to fight
I wish I could make things right
Because now we're just kites

I'm crumbling, spinning, swallowed
My feet underneath, crying from the defeat
She's probably just fine
Drinking the same, my favorite wine
with some other guy

I don't see the girl who promised to love me,
be there for me no matter what
I see cold, dead eyes
Maybe I pushed her too far away
Maybe she could come back one day

Maybe I broke her heart too lightly
Maybe it shattered into pieces
She crumbled & stopped breathing
But maybe she felt nothing

Maybe it was never meant to be
But for me, it was

Simran Kalita

My Kind of Love

Everybody says that the man who wins my heart will be the
luckiest person on this planet
Everybody says that I just need to wait and watch, and one
day, the one will surely come
Everybody says it, so it must be true

But what about all the times I waited and watched, and he
who vied for me moved on to someone else
What about when other people seem to easily find someone
to love
What about me, who has a different kind of love

A kind of love that knows no history, for maybe it is of a
different era
A type of love that can suffer for decades to reunite with
someone, a love that would only recite one name bowing
down to God
A love that doesn't exist in this modern age

My mother raised me to believe in the Romeo-Juliet type of
love, the Heer-Ranjha type of love, the Laila-Majnu type of
love
My mother raised me to be the type of girl who dreams of
star-crossed love that reaches past lifetimes and generations
My mother raised me to be the type of girl who visits the
temple to make prayers every day for someone she's never
even seen or met

You must think I'm crazy
And so would I, if only I could see reality past the
devotional scarf that blinds me
I dream of a type of love that will one day save me, will
save me from this cruel punishment of having the same
dream over and over again

Of a faceless, nameless, solace of a man, who I am, until
now, robbed of knowing the identity
I dream of a man who is the answer to all my blessings
And of course, people will tell me that I should give myself
that love, to stop looking for that love

But what can I do
When I was small, I was told to dream
And I dreamed of so many things, all of which I will
accomplish, but this was my very first dream

I am told my love will not last, that it will fizzle away
I believe that love never dies; it is only our spirit
When my love has the power to protect and encourage, no
one can call it a weakness

I dream of a love that will be our first
I dream of a love that forms before touch, for I have saved
that right for that man as well
And in a world where we have the freedom to love a
million times, to love different people again and again, to
find comfort in letting so many love us, I still have to say
that no one else can measure up

I dream of a love that doesn't ask for a name nor a body, a
love that is so holy so timeless and devoted it is only
between two souls

My kind of love maybe doesn't exist
My kind of love is seen as a fake sickness
My kind of love is the only one that I'll ever accept

Simran Kalita

Is she

Is she really hot or does she just
have long, flowing ebony-colored hair, with knots & curls
in just the right seams,
eyes that capture the depth of all your untold secrets & the
reflection of your smile,
lips that keep pursed within them a thousand adventures
you wish you could behold,
a laugh that evaporates your doubts into the sunset,
overlooking the ocean,
a smile that promises boundless happiness & seeks to
imprison,
conversation that fades into the night, causing you to worry
you've spent every second in her intoxication, yet it's still
not enough,
the familiar nod to make you feel home, as though she
never left and was always there,
fire that reminds you of your mortality, your weakness,
your powerlessness before her,
the sweetness in her voice is fireflies & honey on a warm
summer's twilight,
love that knows no boundaries, no exceptions, no
conditions, no secrets,
an aura that gives you comfort—you're finally found
drifting at sea by a mermaid?

The Poet Inside Me

My favorite sweater

You picked me up
By the side of the street where I wish you were
You called me last night
Said it wouldn't work, your meeting got pulled forward

You were my favorite sweater
Before the loss and the trying and the pushing and the
crying
When things would crumble, the memory of you was
enough
Now that you're here and you're real, I no longer see the
possibilities of you and I
Now that you're human, you're no longer the king of the
castle I drew you up to be

You can't fill the holes in your armor with beautiful gold
anymore
Your eyes have gone black, no space for the stars to hold
anymore
Your touch is nonexistent, and I don't have that kind of
time
Your words may be hopeful, but I don't own the same heart

You were my favorite sweater
When all the world's wind blew and our small city froze
over
You were the only thing that could keep me warm
Now that the thread is loose and the colors are faded
There are too many rips in the fabric to fix anymore
And I just threw out my sewing kit

Simran Kalita

Your vibrant multicolor threads have lost their impact
Your softness has turned to an incessant itch I don't have
the patience for anymore
Your lips don't taste the same, just like your sweater has
started to shrink
It barely fits anymore

I'm sorry to do this to you
This can't be a long exchange of apologies every weekend
Refusing to give you my time of day, because that's what
everyone says
I'm over this, I'm out of here
I've outgrown you, I almost tore you

You were my favorite sweater
But now I just don't wear you anymore

You've lost me forever

And it doesn't matter that there's a string of magnets
holding us apart
I will fight with what's left in me to never go looking for
you again
Unless you run to me

Simran Kalita

Aces

You simply don't know
The hate you inflict
With every unkind word
With every cruel smile

You simply don't know
The way your words dictate the way I perceive you
With every bored look
With every fleeting emotion

You've built a castle made of pencils and erasers
A treasure chest of knowledge
Based on what you think you know the world thinks
But I see through it all

I see through your defensive fortress
I see through your scared eyes
I saw through the world's hatred
I saw through my own disbelief

You're living in a world
Where you think you know everything
Think you know what's best
But you can't even see
The world falling apart around you
And your own juvenile reflection on the wall

Why was I a target
Why does everyone think it was I who did you wrong
Middle school was too young for you to break my heart
Especially when I welcomed you in as my friend
Just for you to bully me instead

The Poet Inside Me

Who do you think you are
To let me accept your flaws and your lines
To let yourself befriend me and hold my hand
Only to trample around the earth finding all the faults
Forming your own opinions
Breaking my heart
Breaking everyone's heart
Who the hell do you think you are

You will never know and you may never know
Because I am just too good at hiding it all
Behind this fake visage that I have painted over my
disheartened face
You think you know, don't you
But you will never know
And I will never let you

Hiya

I say hi

You say no

Before I breathe
A breath

You leave your
Home

Away
Far away

From the fields
That protected us

Covered us in the storm
Underneath we slept
Away from the hunters

That captured us tonight

I say hi

You say yes

Then I die.

Dream

It was an inexplicable feeling.
There was so much chaos and hunger and war.
And then he told me it would all be okay.
And that I was safe.
He would protect me.

His soothing voice numbed my every emotion,
while his very touch to stroke my hair awakened passion.
And then he locked me in his arms like a songbird in a
cage.
And I felt the warmth I had been yearning for since I was a
little girl.
And the whole world seemed to drift away for a second,
as I slept peacefully in his embrace.

Dreams take you to a whole other galaxy,
Where your deepest, darkest thoughts are unveiled.
Over the soundless sky and past the shiny night stars,
There is a jungle I never thought to discover.
Underneath the heavy clouds and behind the forest,
There is a meadow where I'll meet you.
Grazing my skin, you'll smile at me because
Here is where dreams cross the lining into a euphoric
reality.

Simran Kalita

Faaslon (Translated: Distances)

We're all only passengers boarded on this train going in different directions. We don't cross paths, and we don't talk amongst each other. We are simply existing. You're my passenger. We're all passengers.

Placeholder

Look me in the eyes
And tell me all your lies
Tell me what was real
Tell me what wasn't

I followed you through the empty park
Blindly, listening to only my heart
With a haste because a dagger sat in my chest
Clung to whom I thought was a friend

I followed a light when all I saw was dark
After the painful betrayal of the man I thought I loved
The first guy I would've brought to see my dad
I fell in love with his brain

You were just a placeholder
A simple passerby
When I lost my magnet
You were there to link on to in exchange

I fooled you with my eyes
I fooled myself searching for him in yours
I'm not sorry because you turned your back on me
But all along you were equivalent to air

I could've drawn a face with curly hair on my palms
And at least he'd be there
You weren't up for the job, and you never will be
You were just another body to love

Another body I thought I could call mine
A body I thought I could surrender myself to
A heart that played like a song on loop in my head
A smile that gave me too many dreams to count, but I want
to forget

You were just a placeholder
The next guy in line at the coffee shop
The only male specimen left to date
You weren't even worthy

You were just another option
I knew I could get you; it wasn't a challenge
I rolled the dice on a game and pretended to play
When all along I knew things would end the same way

You were just a placeholder
Your heart was on the line
I lost mine a while ago
When I gave up everything to save my soul

You were just a placeholder
Those sweet words I whispered into your ears
Lying because I cared for you
Don't you know that I regret being there for you

I thought maybe I'd be riddled with guilt
If I left when the fire started in your bedroom
I let it spread to the kitchen then I locked myself in
I let the kerosene take away the ashes from your touch

You were just a placeholder
A pillowcase to bury my head into
The words you said I thought were my own
Let myself believe you needed me, I needed you

The Poet Inside Me

You were just a placeholder
And now I have a vacancy
Now I have to find someone else
To replace the hole the placeholder left in me

K—

Why we never would've worked:

I would've given up everything for you
    , but
        you would've given me up for everything.

Turn back time

I loved you for three years
I waited for you for one
I prayed for you still, every single day
And then you went and fell in love with someone else
instead.

Drift

Drift away
All you can do is leave
Go on
Do your magic
And I'll sip the poison as I watch you go

I want you to leave
I want you to stay
I can't make up my mind
But when you're near me
You're my favorite song
And I'm addicted to your rhythm

You're a magnet inching closer to my helix
I'm on this gas that makes me hurt
You make me hurt
But you make me loved

And as our loving bodies wrap around each other
You seal the night with one last kiss
Before you drift away to come back again

You and I

What you and I had was
Magical, irrational
And dysfunctional

You try and run and hide
While I still hold you tight
You whisper threats and glare
I try not to be aware

Of what you couldn't say to me
And it's so easy to be
Happy, won't you let me be happy?

'Cause now I'm looking out my window
Waiting for him to pick me up
And he promises things just like you did
The only underlying factor
That makes me more and more attracted
He keeps his word.

Simran Kalita

Hope starts with a 'you'

You puzzle me, you came from no where
Probably because you were always here

You know me, I know you
And probably because I know you so well
I just know I'd never want to ruin this

You're so unlike the others, the ones who had me
questioning my sanity
You're like a warm, tight hug

But I know I'm not falling in love

It's just that I talk to you everyday
And you listen to all the things I have to say
And you tell me about your life
But I'd never imagine being your wife

Meeting you makes me believe in friendship
Talking to you makes me want a bond like this
But with someone else
Listening to your stories makes my own feel heard

When I think about you,
from my mouth escapes a little giggle

Because I was almost about to tell you
what my dad said about finding love
But you distracted me instead
with a stupid little comment

Oh, you

The Poet Inside Me

You're unbelievable
And any girl would be lucky to have you

You were there when I didn't even want myself anymore
You pick up every time I call
You always let me through your walls

I feel like you're falling
Please reassure me you're not falling
I couldn't face breaking your heart
So I tread a very careful line
Pretend to ignore the cheeky things you say
Because I know I make you feel a certain way

I know even if you find the perfect girl
You might reconsider if you'd have to leave my world

So I give you my support in every endeavor
So you don't feel like I'm your lover

Believe me, I know how much you want to find that love
And I'm the same, it seems our lives might be intertwined

But always keeping you at an arm's distance
can't be good for my health

Always stopping right before I cross the line
can't be good for your heart

This is my first poem about you.
I hope we never grow apart

Sticky

You're stuck, sticking on me like a drug
But is this passion now my paradise?
Or are you really a refusing-to-leave parasite
ew

Aren't you tired of running around your own ball games?
Who wins, because I'm sure it's not you
Not even anyone you take back with you

Not even the one you're feeling up in her home
I hope you can make either of you happy
Because you'll never be happy
As long as I love you

But the moment I don't, oh
How you'll fall
You're already on the ground
running around thinking you've accomplished something

I hope you're sick in your own daydreams
Matter of fact, I hope you never dream
I hope I don't hope anything for you anymore

Because that is the last straw before it all falls

Does her skin peel so smoothly underneath your fingertips?
Does her scent fill every corner of your brain
Does her laughter and love make you want to keep going
Does she feel you the way I feel you
Do you fill her up the way you wish you could do me

How boring of you
You're no special, doing exactly what every other one is
expected of
You're not even rare, how sour when I taste the thought of
you
I need to chase it with a cold tequila shot, and I hate tequila
But you know, you always like sweet things

And I'm the sweetest
Sickly sweet
So sweet you sneezed all over the place
Sick from the love bug I gave you

How sad for you
Clean up your sticky mess, loser

Simran Kalita

Who is she

Was she worth it?
Was she

Does she smell the way I do
Does she taste the way I do
Does she dance the way I do

Are her eyes as pretty as mine
Is her hair softer than mine
Does she look better in a bathing suit

You always used to come around, tell me I was your all

It's 2am now
And I can't sleep

Because all I can dream about is you dreaming about her

Are her eyes just the shade of blue we watched the night
sky turn into
Is it the same blue where our oceans don't meet
Or the color of the jacket that you stole

Is her hair the golden you wish all your jewelry was made
of
Is it the same vibrance as the sunset we missed
Or is it the same shade you saw on that one strand of my
hair

Does she hold your hand the way I never got to
Does she laugh at your jokes that we both know aren't
funny
Does she listen to your stories and all your insecurities

The Poet Inside Me

Has she seen the smile you saved for me
Or the little notes I wrote to you
The songs that had your name in them

Did she spend the night bathing in the moonlight
Talking by the candlelight
Tells you to have a safe flight

I'm losing more and more of myself
As I imagine you filling yourself up with more and more of
her
Is she the dream you've been chasing

I was never enough was I
I was never even in the picture
I never will be

I'm too mean aren't I, too real
I'm too different aren't I
I don't fit in, too complicated to have me around

Grieving the love I never received
Stalking the way you never missed a single thing she did,
not even when you were with me
None of it was real with me

There's a picture of her and I, you know
And she looks oh so pretty, so flawless
But I'm no less a diamond next to her

Cubic zirconia
I don't want to tear her down
She doesn't deserve that

Simran Kalita

But do you know her, and does she know you
The way that I do
Let me believe that she doesn't

Because if not you, then no one
And if not me, then who can
Love you the way that I do

Does she even know
Do you even realize
Who I am, who is she to you

Like a madman
I set out to win your heart
When it was already taken by anyone other than me

Why are things so unfair
In love and loss
I give up, for the hundredth time

Just saying

I found love every time I looked at you
I looked for you in every boy I saw
You left me to find something you're looking for
I hope you find me in every girl you're looking at

Simran Kalita

Soulmate

He looks at me with his dark, peering eyes
He laughs at all of my jokes
His hand moves to engulf mine, cold to the touch
He makes everything *better*.

As I look back into the narrow tunnels through his eyes,
I see a man I feel like I have known my entire life
And yet, there is a strange disconnect.

Something about the timing, or about the air.
My nimble hands can't quite put a finger on it.

He crosses off every section in my stupid list.
The way he touches my lips, my hands, my soul
Just takes me away.

I don't think I really love him, and
I don't think I want to.

I feel like I've been thrown into this hole
Where I never wanted to be in in the first place.

It's complicated, not just rough around the edges.
And it engulfs me with a feeling, but it feels
More like poison. I'm struggling to climb out.

He isn't the same soul divided into two, and
He isn't the perfect puzzle piece to my missing half

I am whole, or at least I wanted to be
Until you came along

I feel a strange connection, but at the same time
He isn't at all what I wanted him to be

The Poet Inside Me

And I regret, and I curse, and I throw it all

I am so fucking done with falling for whom
My heart decides for me

Do you think I asked for this? To fall in love
with my best friend in people?

I wanted to reject it so bad, but then there's
something tugging at my heart strings,
and I know it's you

And I want to turn around and hold you in my arms
so badly, but I just can't because I don't really want you
I didn't really choose you

The universe chose you for me, and now for some
godforsaken reason, I have to pay the price for it?

Why can't you? I don't understand how this story's
been written, but I want a different, proper ending

I don't want a soulmate.

Simran Kalita

Franchise

It's a franchise
It's a gold mine
What we made our minds into

What we follow
What we pray
What we admire
What we are devoted to

And Isn't it not What someone
Else had constructed

You aren't even original
Enough to show your face
Hiding behind that name,
that word, that place, that
Franchise

But we can't go against it either
Dear

So what to do
Continue
Commence
And be thrown off your
Pedestal

You can't even win so
Don't even try

Ghar (Translated: Home)

Let's go back
To the place where I felt home under the scrapes of what
was left behind
Take a trip back to my old country
I don't know how far I strayed
Will you come with me
Because I feel home within your fingertips
I feel comfort within the confines of your arms
I feel pleasure under your delicate hands
You've wrapped around me like a cursive line
You make me feel like poetry
You trace me like a shadow drawing
Written from the leather notebook of a Spanish song
Your sloppy kisses on my face remind me of when I was a
young girl
To be wanted by you is to be taken
Like a little girl whose face is pressed up against the
window of a candy shop
You offer me joy at last
I was craving
To go back home
And now I return to you

California

I don't know what brought me to you
But I never wish to be parted from you
I'm obsessed in a way that can't be expressed in syllables
They fall too short

Your warm weather, your calm breeze
Your ease of life
You feel like home

A day spent well feels like a year
A year I spent brings me to tears
No fragment of time is enough but even a second is a
worthwhile moment
There's nothing that makes me happier

I can cut ties with people
I can cut ties with things that meant so much before
But I can't bring myself to cut ties with this land

This magic, this feeling of nostalgia wrapped in summer,
presented as a beach flower
Your desert, your vast valleys
Your boundlessness
Your hopes and dreams that you carry

Everyone visits you but no one knows you through and
through
I'd be lying if I even ventured to try
I love you so
I love you so

My sweet, sweet Cali
My little love
The place that offered shelter when there was nothing but a
storm
The place that tried to make me smile even when all I saw
was rain clouds

I could never part from you
I could never be far from you

Simran Kalita

Extraordinary

The power of the pen is so extraordinary I never thought I could do this all the magic that lies within these tiny hands reaching up to touch the sky although the night stars are out and the storm is near and the whole world is gone away in hiding still I reach the way nobody has ever reached to fly as high as nobody has ever flown and I stretch my fingers caressing the cool air hoping and waiting for something to happen but nothing ever does and so I lie awake underneath the sky on the naked grass where my feet are pressed so tight they feel the ants crawl across my skin yet still I try and I try and I reach and I fly and I see something extraordinary.

The Chase

I'm gonna run
I'm not looking back
Far away
To a corner of this earth where no one can find me
No one can see me, no one can feel me

I was looking for home
For so long
Hoping it lay within your touch
Praying that the way you looked at me was because you
needed me
And now I feel more lost than ever

Your love blinds you
You think it's powerless standing next to me
You know the ways that I move you, but you wonder if I
will fool you
Your love is strong
But you are weak

My love blinds me too
It thinks you are nothing but golden and marble
A sight to be in awe of
I didn't realize how much we are the same but all the ways
that we differ
I am strong, but my love for you makes me weak

I feel this play in my bones
Written and rewritten and unwritten but still going strong
Every time I take a pill, I picture myself swallowing a dose
of you
Why do I know your love is strong enough to cure me?
I've decided to run away

I won't let you see me
I won't let you feel me
I won't let your hands heal me
I won't even allow you to speak to me

There is not a land I can run to fast enough to keep us apart
But the oceans that separate us must divide in order for you
to find me
I am trying to hide
I am keeping myself from you

There is not a place far enough for me to disappear to
Where even the darkness is confounded by me
Where shadows don't recognize me
And the sun's rays search for me all day
The stars call out to no answer

I want to disappear
And let no one remember me when I am back
Because no one knows who she was
Only your hands had the fortune of coming so close
Let me go

Do not run after me.

Leaving without a goodbye

I couldn't take it anymore
And I wanted to stop caring
I wanted my heart to believe what my head was saying,
what you were telling me
I wanted to be free of you

Free from your thoughts
From your memories, from the things you told me
I needed to learn how to forget when all I ever did was
clutch onto what I had of you
And I'm sorry if that's crazy

I chose radio silence
I chose to never reply
I chose to not let you have a single part of me if you didn't
want all of me
I chose to keep you away

I chose to keep every path that led you to me untraceable
Because I always chose you
I told you I was done caring, that I never waited for you
But boy did I lie

I told you I was fine, when it felt like my heart had been
ripped out of its place
I told you that I was already over it, even though you could
see the pain the last time that I saw you
It killed me to choose not to talk to you
It kills me to know that you know that now

I'm hurt and embarrassed, and I never should've been
It hurts more to think you have no idea why
Maybe my words were always deceiving
And you never understood who I actually am

I fell in love with you long before you ever could've
thought I would
At the worst possible time for the both of us
From that moment, everything you did and said had a
newfound meaning
And every time you made a mistake, I crumbled a little bit

Too late did I realize that I had fallen in love
And I didn't do anything to stop it
But what even is love
Because I've never felt it before, and maybe the idea of you
is what I love instead

I do love you as a person, my friend
But I also loved the thought that you could be everything
And it would be so easy
Because you already know me, and trust me, no one else
does

Maybe I was settling or taking up a challenge
But at the end of the day, you were what I wanted
And the thought kills me that you never actually felt that
way
All my effort was of no avail

I should've seen reason long ago instead of giving you
endless chances
You unknowingly stole my heart with each lasso
From making me feel smart and beautiful and talented
To giving me things only a lover would

You kept saying things that I thought meant more than just
words
And you would look at me in ways that made me blush
And it didn't help that your friends knew who I was, or that
he hung out the whole night with us
How could I have been so stupid

Maybe because I loved you
Everything you did was granted a hallway pass
And even though you came to my birthdays,
They never should've ended with just us

I was in love with you
Obviously I would choose to be with you
But then what is your excuse
And how come you never touched me, but I still feel used

I would rather you have touched me, had your way with me
Can't you tell that no one else has before
And, even today, the closest I have come to sleeping with
someone
Is when you woke up next to me the night I turned twenty

Yes, it's true
Because I always wanted it to be you
But what a fool I was
Especially when I blamed myself for putting those pillows
between us

You must think I'm crazy
And I won't fault you for thinking
When everything you did, you did carelessly
But everything I did was in the lens of someone who truly
never lived until she left for college

You often wonder in amazement
How I came to be
Well, the truth is, I spent most of my life surrounded by my
own thoughts, my own demons, my own art
I never knew I had talent until you said so, every trick I
pulled was because you enjoyed the show

You love my painting, you love my poems
You love my songs, but did you ever stop to wonder
Where the inspiration came from
You are behind everything, and it's because you're all I've
ever known

It's not like I thought you were perfect
I knew you had flaws but I was ready to love all of you
And looking at all the things I've written about, they are
only half-true
Some of my poems are from dreams, my imagination, or
embellishing things with other guys, but the other half is
you

Of course I've liked many guys before and after you
But the difference is your being, your friendship, and your
goals
I wanted you the way I wanted all of them combined
And the fact that you knew me so well and still chose to
stick around made me feel special

Yes, I was broken
I'm not afraid to admit
The things that have happened in my life left me a person
with a lot of things I needed to fix
But now that that I feel whole, it intrigues me how you're
still stuck like a statue everywhere I go

I didn't even leave you with a goodbye
I decided I have nothing left to say to you in this lifetime
I left in a gradual decline, focusing more on me and what I
would do with my life
And I thought I would never see you again

How could I face you
How could I look you in those eyes
How could I sit across from you the way we usually do and
pretend everything was alright
I'm not good at confrontation, and you scare me to pieces

How could I digest the truth or hide the embarrassment in
my eyes
When all along I thought you were trying to tell me
something
Just for you to tell me I am blind
Weren't you the one who told me I deserve better

I should've known from that one sentence
But weren't you the one who also promised to be better for
me and said I meant more than others
Weren't you the one who started picking out romantic
restaurants and texting me that you were thankful for me
You were the first person who ever said "I love you" to
me—the first person I was ever able to say it back to—just
to find out it was only as a friend

Every time I told you I liked you
I meant that I loved you
And you have no idea the amount of courage it took, only
to be rejected every single time
But each time, you would come back and give me reasons
to say it again

Simran Kalita

I guess I'm really good at talking
Because I convinced you I was okay
I convinced you I was even better without you
And that I was catering to many others instead

Well, though I kept my options open, I also held a candle
for you
So much so that everybody who I love knows your name
And it's crazy how you threw that in my face
Among many other things that I fault you for doing to a girl
who loved you, and you had no intentions of going through
with

You've made many mistakes yourself
And I guess you'll never admit
You made me think I was lying, and you know I never lie
I don't get why you kept coming back to me and made me
feel like you didn't like seeing me with other guys

Now I'm obviously the crazy one
The one who wanted to give everything to someone who
gave nothing and wants nothing
Why are you a parasite in my life
And why am I still tormented by your presence and
non-presence in my life

I think you're diabolical for the way you broke my heart
Slowly and crushing even the little pieces, bit by bit
And the best part is you're exempt from the blame of it
I can't even be mad because I know you were suffering
from a broken heart yourself

But then why was I a target
Why oh why, is the way I ask god
And I cry and say it's not fair to have played me this way
Am I stupid, am I really just insane

Don't you think it hurts me to not see you anymore
To realize that maybe the last time you saw me was the last
time we might ever see each other
That the last time we would talk would be so many months
ago
And that even though I only knew you for four years,
somehow it felt like you recognized my soul

Now even though I am no longer in love with you
Don't you know it still hurts to see you happy without me,
knowing that you probably don't even miss me
Knowing that maybe you'll paint me out to be a fool
But I also know you, and so I know you would never do
that

Don't you think it's maddening that I'm sitting here trying
to convince myself that you're the bad guy
When, to be honest, you are, but I also know how much
you really do love me
Don't you know I know that you miss me
Don't you know I know that you don't hate me or fault me
for falling for you

But admitting it was in my head would be wrong because
of all the times you said things that no one else would say
Exactly what my heart would want you to say
For someone who believes in signs, everything felt like a
sign
And the feeling I got sitting across from you made me feel
like some strange connection tied the both of us with a
string

Maybe you feel this way or don't
But let me believe that you don't
And that every time you shared a piece of your life with me
was because I was just a mirror
Holding up the reflection of someone else you wished was
there instead

After all these things, I still understand if you don't get why
I fell for you
But please don't let me have any more pieces of you
I don't want to love you, and I clearly can't separate a lover
from a friend
You once held my heart, and what was left unsaid has been
said

I promise you I will find my way back to you eventually
Just let me fall in love with someone else in peace
I loved you too much to ever let go of you
But you know, I've mastered the art of loving you without
you even being here

It's the way I always could feel when you were upset
And that, to me, was a clear indication that something was
happening between us
But now that I know it's not, I'm glad at least I'll be able to
sense you even when you're god knows how many miles
away
And if you ever miss me, then just close your eyes, and I'll
be there

What hurts me the most is the conversation we had over text
Two years ago, when I first told you I had feelings for you, but you were going through it
How could you expect a girl to get over her first love so easily
You didn't even love yourself, when I loved you in a way where I wanted to take all your pain away

I loved you in a way that I thought you were made of gold and would always be worthy
I loved you in a way where I was confused how you couldn't love you because I loved you so unconditionally
I loved you in a way where I fought to understand what could make you not love your reflection, who you are, your personality
I loved you in a way that, despite any pain you could ever cause me, I would still wrap you in my love for centuries

And now I love you in a way where I want to love someone else one day
Not as friends but as lovers, and a little bit of time before as strangers
There's no way I thought I could ever say goodbye—not when we know this much about each other
And now I love you in a way where I finally say goodbye—I hope you read this and know that it might not be forever

I'll love you in a way where we might one day again see each other.

Special selection (Hindi/Urdu)

you + i are...

Poetry

rozana aya karo
hamaare saath baitha karo
thoda hans toh lo

hazaaron meel door ka hai yeh
dhaaga hamaare darmiyaan

bin shabd.
andekha

bilkul sangeet ki tarah

kabhi aya toh karo
roz hamaari galiyon mein

khair chhodiye

humko aankhon ki zaroorat nahi
aapko pehchaanne ke liye

saans ki zaroorat nahi
aapko mehsoos karne ke liye

dil ki zaroorat nahi
aapki har dhadkan ko samajhne ke liye

kaisa rishta hai yeh
bin alfaaz
bin baatein
bin yaadein

sirf ek hi pehchaan hai in faaslon ke liye

Simran Kalita

(Translated)

come to see me every day
take a seat with me
laugh a little

this thread between us
it stretches across thousands of miles

wordless
unseen

just like music

do come over some time
wander through our streets every day

well, never mind

i don't need eyes
to recognize you

no need for senses
to feel your presence

no need for a heart
to understand your every heartbeat

what kind of bond is this
without words
without conversation
without memories

only one identity exists for these distances

.

Tumse milke

O pyaar karne wale
Yeh kya jaadu kar gaye
Kyun Rab se mujhe chura liya
Kyun khud se mujhe chura liya
Kya hai ki ab sirf tumhari neeli aankhon mein
Meri khud ki parchaayi nazar aati hai
Kal jab tum aaye, tumhare saath
Chaand aaya, taare khile, roshni aayi
Ab agar tum jaaoge
Toh chup-chup ke main bhi tumhare peeche chalungi
Phoolon ke rang bas tum hi laa sakte ho
Baadal ki barsaat bas tum hi laa sakte ho
Mujhe chhod ke mat jaana
Zyada waqt ke liye
O humsafar
Ab se, tum mere ban chuke ho
Aur hum hum ban chuke hain

Simran Kalita

(Translated)
Meeting you

O beloved
What magic have you cast
Why did you steal me from God
Why have I lost myself to you
Why is it that now only in your blue eyes
I can see my own reflection
Yesterday when you came, with you
Came the moon, the stars bloomed, & light followed
Now if you leave
Then quietly I'll follow the steps in your direction
Only you can bring color to the flowers
Only you can summon rain from the clouds
Don't leave me behind
For too long
O companion
From this moment you have become mine
And we have become us

Seher

Jannat uski baahon mein basti hai
Mohabbat uske badan mein theharti hai

(Translated)
Dawn

Heaven resides in her embrace
Love awaits within her body

Everyday

Har din
Tu mera pehla khayaal hai
Har raat
Tu meri aakhri khwahish hai

Kab jaayegi yeh beemaari

(Translated)
Everyday

Every day
You are my first thought
Every night
You are my last desire

When will this sickness leave

The fruit of patience

Uss waqt ka intezaar hai
Jab khuda ki hansi sagar ke shor mein dab jaaye
Uss waqt ka intezaar hai
Jab roshni hazaar meel door se mujhe milne aaye
Uss waqt ka intezaar hai
Jab uska haath tumhare dil par rakhna mujhe takleef na de
Uss waqt ka intezaar hai
Jab jannat ka darwaaza bilkul saamne aaye
Uss waqt ka intezaar hai
Uss lamhe ke liye ruk
Uss aaraam ke liye thehar

Tab milegi khushi, tu nahi, bas main
Neend poori hogi, saansein na rukengi
Uss waqt ka intezaar hai
Intezaar ka phal

(Translated)
The fruit of patience

Waiting for the moment
When god's laughter drowns out in the ocean waves
Waiting for the moment
When sunlight will travel a thousand miles to meet me
Waiting for the moment
When her hand on your heart no longer causes me pain
Waiting for the moment
When the gates of heaven appear right before me
Waiting for the moment
The pause for time
The linger for rest

Then happiness will find me, not you, only me
Sleep will be complete, and breathing will not cease
Waiting for the moment
The fruit of patience

Bahar

Mmmm I'm a caged bird in this chaos
I would spread my wings but they're tied

You enchant me, call me, throw me
I'm a force of nature inside this lamp

So free me, and let me show you the world this can be

I brush my hands across my own palms
Feel my world as it just revolves

I make waves just like the ocean
You can pull, fold me, mold me

But in time, you will see that it's me you will need

Hum bahar
Kidhar jaa rahe hain
Kabhi dekha nahi in vaadiyon ko

Sunn
Yeh dhun pakad mera
Jaa, le kar is jagah se door, mujhe kho jaane de

Aasmaan ki khushi
Raunak ki jalti
Par hum sirf door

Bachpan ki ghadi
Jhulne ki woh hasi
Mere saanson mein tu bana le ghar

Bahar, bahar, bahar, bahar

Simran Kalita

(Translated)
Outside

…

We are outside
Where are we going
I have never seen these valleys before

Listen
Catch this melody of mine
Go, take me far away from this place so I can lose myself

The joy of the sky
The glow of brightness
But we remain distant

Childhood moments
The laughter from swinging
Make a home within my breaths

Outside, outside, outside, outside

Dua

Main tere har saans ki ankahi dua
Main tere har lamhe ki ansuni saza
Main tere aansuon ki dawa,
Tere honthon ki mannat

Mujhe od le, aur main bikhar jaaungi,
Bas iss mulaaqat ko behchaini mein mat rehne de

Simran Kalita

(Translated)
Prayer

I am the unspoken prayer of your every breath
I am the unheard punishment of your every moment
I am the remedy for your tears
The wish on your lips

Wrap me around you, and I will shatter
Just don't let this meeting remain in restlessness

Na-insaafi

Kal agar meri aankhon ko suraj nahi dikhe
Phir bhi tere chehre ke har aansoo ko samajh paaungi
Kal agar mere kaanon ko sangeet nahi sunai de
Phir bhi teri aawaz ko pehchaan lungi
Kal agar iss duniya ki mehek mujhe chhod jaati hai
Phir bhi teri khushboo ko yaad rakhoongi
Kal agar meri zubaan mujhse chhin jaati hai
Phir bhi tere naam ka swaad mere honthon par reh jaayega
Kal agar koi mere haath kaat de
Phir bhi teri har saans ko mehsoos kar paungi

Aisi na-insaafi
Sirf kismetwaalon ko milti hai
Jahaan unke dost sitaare hote hain
Unke dushman kirnon mein rehte hain

Agar shaitaan khud aake mujhse mera dil maang le
Toh mujhe bas tere taraf kadam aage badhana hai
Agar khuda khud mujhse meri zindagi maang le
Toh main tere hi kandhon par rakh ke chale jaaungi

Koi kaaran nahi hai iss paagalpan ka
Kai log ise dhoondte hue phisal gaye ya kho gaye
Samajh jao pyaar hi naam hai iss na-insaafi ka

Simran Kalita

(Translated)
Injustice

If tomorrow my eyes can no longer see the sun
Even then I will understand every tear that streams your
face
If tomorrow my ears can no longer hear music
Even then I will recognize your voice
If tomorrow the fragrance of this world will leave me
Even then I will remember your scent
If tomorrow my tongue is taken from me
Even then the taste of your name will linger on my lips
If tomorrow someone cuts off my hands
Even then I will feel your every breath

Such injustice
Is granted only to the fortunate
Those whose friends are stars
And whose foes dwell in the rays of the sun

If the devil himself comes and asks me for my heart
All I need is to take a step toward you
If God himself comes and asks me for my life
I will leave it on your shoulders and walk away

There is no reason for this madness
Many have stumbled or lost themselves searching for it
Understand that love is the very name of this injustice

Mubarak ho

Mubarak ho, jaanam
Mubarak ho, sanam

Aaj se aap ki Aashiqui aap ki ho chuki hai
Aaj se woh aapke aangan ko sajaa sakti hai
Aaj se uss par aapka haq banta hai

Tamasha kijiye, jaanam
Hungama kijiye, sanam

Aaj se aapka har sapna poora ho chuka hai
Aaj se aapki har khwahish safal ho gayi hai
Aaj se aapke baahon se tanhayi mit chuki hai

Shehnayi bajaiye, jaanam
Tareekh nikaaliye, sanam

Aaj se aapke Chandni aapki ho chuki hai
Aaj se aapke dhadkan ko dhun mili hai
Aaj se aapke chahne wali khud ko kho chuki hai

Simran Kalita

(Translated)
Congratulations

Congratulations, my love
Congratulations, beloved

From today onwards your love belongs to you
From today she can decorate your steps
From today onwards she is rightfully yours

Put on a spectacle, my love
Create commotion, beloved

From today onwards all your dreams have been fulfilled
From today onwards all your desires have come true
From today the loneliness has vanished from your arms

Play music, my love
Mark the date, beloved

From today onwards your Chandni (moonlight) is yours
From today onwards your heartbeat has found its melody
From today your love has lost herself to you

Hawale aapke

Yeh aankhen, tere hawale
Yeh honth, tere hawale
Yeh muskaan, tere hawale
Yeh hasi, tere hawale
Yeh khushboo, tere hawale
Yeh haath, tere hawale
Yeh zulfein, tere hawale
Yeh baahein, tere hawale
Yeh badan, tere hawale
Woh saaya, tere hawale
Yeh dil, tere hawale
Har dhadkan, tere hawale
Har sapna, tere hawale
Har khayaal, tere hawale
Sab tere hawale
Hum tere hawale
Kya aap mere hawale hain?

Simran Kalita

(Translated)
Entrusted to you

These eyes, entrusted to you
These lips, entrusted to you
This smile, entrusted to you
This laughter, entrusted to you
This fragrance, entrusted to you
These hands, entrusted to you
These tresses, entrusted to you
These arms, entrusted to you
This body, entrusted to you
That shadow, entrusted to you
This heart, entrusted to you
Each heartbeat, entrusted to you
Every dream, entrusted to you
Every thought, entrusted to you
Everything, entrusted to you
I am entrusted to you
Are you entrusted to me?

Yeh Sheher

Yeh darmiyan kidhar chala
Teri khushboo jo hawa mein basa
Kyun door itne
Kal tere saaye ko maine dekha
Yaadein teri nahi chhoot ti hain
Taaron se kyun itne door

Har lafz tujhe keh doo abhi
Jo tab mujhe nahi aaya tha ehsaas
Mujhe sab yaad hai
Jab hum dono khelte the din bar din
Kaash main tere saath hoti

Main naachun deewani si tere hi saath
Sab raaste main jaungi tere liye
Bas ek hi sach hai tujhe main kahoon
Har manzil hai tu hi tu

Kal tujhe dekha tha akele nahi
Hamari mohabbat adhoori rahi
Yeh mushkil sadi
Khush kaun hai abhi

Har lafz tujhe keh doon abhi
Jo tab mujhe nahi aaya tha ehsaas
Mujhe sab yaad hai
Jab hum dono khelte the din bar din
Kaash main tere saath hoti

Main naachun deewani si tere hi saath
Sab raaste main jaungi tere liye
Bas ek hi sach hai tujhe main kahoon
Har manzil hai tu hi tu

Simran Kalita

(Translated)
This Town — inspired by Niall Horan's song

Where did this distance go away to
Your fragrance that remains in the air
Why so far away
Yesterday I saw your shadow
Your memories don't fade
Why so far away from the stars

Every word I want to say to you now
That never occurred to me back then
I remember everything
When we used to play day after day
I wish I were with you

I dance like I'm crazy just with you
I'd take every path for you
There's only one truth I will tell you
Every destination is you, only you

Yesterday I saw that you weren't alone
Our love remains incomplete
These difficult times
Who is happy now

Every word I want to say to you now
That never occurred to me back then
I remember everything
When we used to play day after day
I wish I were with you

I dance like I'm crazy just with you
I'd take every path for you
There's only one truth I will tell you
Every destination is you, only you

Tere aane se main behchain rahoon
Titliyaan ud jaati hain jab tu aata
Bas ek hi sach hai tujhe main kahoon
Sirf ek manzil tu hi tu

Yeh waqt hai mushkil
Main thehraa hoon
Par aaj tujhe dekh ke

Main naachun deewani si tere hi saath
Sab raaste main jaungi tere liye
Bas ek hi sach hai tujhe main kahoon
Har manzil hai tu hi tu

Tere aane se main behchain rahoon
Titliyaan ud jaati hain jab tu aata
Bas ek hi sach hai tujhe main kahoon
Sirf ek manzil tu hi tu

Simran Kalita

Your arrival leaves me restless
Butterflies take flight when you come near
There's only one truth I want to tell you
You are my only destination, only you

This time is difficult
I stand still
But seeing you today

I dance like I'm crazy just with you
I'll take every path for you
There's only one truth I will tell you
Every destination is you, yes you

Your arrival leaves me restless
Butterflies begin to fly when you come
There's only one truth I want to tell you
Every destination is you, only you

Gussa

Gussa feel kar rahi ho?
Toh gussa feel karo na yaar
Kitne der tak apne jazbaat aur apne aap ko chhupakar
rahogi?
Tum insaan ho, insaan bano. Insaan jaise hasso, insaan jaise
raho, insaan jaise naaraz ho, insaan jaise chillaao. Paagal
bano, par apne aap ko dabaa ke mat rakhna. Bas mehsoos
karte rehna.

(Translated)
Anger

Are you feeling angry?
Then let yourself feel angry, dude
How long will you hide your feelings, hide yourself?
You are human, be human. Laugh like a human, live like a
human, be upset like a human, scream like a human. Go
crazy, but don't keep suppressing yourself. Just keep
feeling.

Notions

Rabba
Mujhe chhod de
Kya gunaah kiya hai maine
Iss pyaar ko qubool karke

Naaraz nahi hoon main
Haar gayi hoon tujhse
Meri jaan, mera pyaar
Meri kavita

Waapas nahi jaa sakti main
Baabul ke aangan mein
Kho gayi hoon apne khaabon mein
Toot gayi hoon main

Simran Kalita

(Translated)

Oh God
Let me go
What sin have I committed
By accepting this love

I am not upset
I've lost to you
My beloved, my love
My poem

I cannot return
To my father's house
I am lost in my dreams
I am broken

Piya o mere piya

Piya ko main kyun boloon
Main kya boloon
Kis mooh se boloon

Haye, mann aur tann ki
Behchaini hamesha se thi
Piya ko main kyun boloon

Piya ke hone se
Hulchul hoti hai
Piya ko main kyun boloon

Kaise main boloon
Ki mujhe aisa laga ki piya mujhe chahte hain
Khair, piya ko main kya boloon

Simran Kalita

(Translated)
Beloved o my beloved

Why should I speak to my beloved
What should I say
With what face should I say it

Oh, the restlessness
Of the heart and soul has always been there
Why should I speak to my beloved

With the presence of my beloved
There's a stir within
Why should I speak to my beloved

How should I say
That I felt as if my beloved loves me
Well, what should I say to my beloved

Nahi bol payi

Nahi bol payi
Uss chaand ko
Jiske taraf har nazar padti hai

Woh chamakta chaand
Jiske upar humne dil lutaya
Kaash unki nazar hum par hoti

Main ek taara banke pari hoon
Aur jab band darwazon ke kamre mein hoon
Mere par udte hain

Kaash wo chaand yeh dekh pata
Iss jaadoo ko jab bhi raat hoti hai
Ki main bas unka ho jati hoon

Aur ek pal ke liye main bhi pari ban jaati hoon
Mere bhi par udte hain
Aur main bhi ek chamakta tara hoon

Nahi bol payi
Kyun boloon uss chaand se
Jisne kabhi mujh par nazar hi nahi daali

Simran Kalita

(Translated)
I couldn't say it

I couldn't say it
To that moon
Towards whom every gaze turns

That shining moon
Whom I have lost my heart to
If only his gaze had fallen upon me

I am an angel disguised as a star
And when I'm in a room with closed doors
My wings take flight

If only that moon could see
This magic every time night falls
How I become his and his alone

And for a moment, I become an angel
My wings take flight
And I, too, become a shining star

I couldn't say it
Why should I speak to the moon
Who has never even noticed me

Ab kya

Ab tumhe pata hai ki main tumse kitna pyaar karti thi
Jab tumne mujhe ek boond bhi nahi diya
Aur maan lo
Ki tumse zyada pyaar aur koi nahi kar sakta hai
Lekin aazma ke dekh lo
Ki agar maine tumse itni mohabbat ki
Toh uske liye main kya kar sakti hoon
Jo mujhe woh pyaar dega
Aakhir afsos ki baat hai
Ki tum mujhse sab kuch maang lete
Toh main khushi se de deti
Magar tum yeh pehchaan na sake
Aur tumhara har maang kam par jaata
Toh ab jaante ho ki sirf main tumhe itna pyaar de sakti thi
Lekin ek hai jo mujhe sabse zyada pyaar karega
Mere jaisa
Aur agar maine tumse itna pyaar kiya
Toh socho usse kitna pyaar karungi
Aazma ke dekh lo.

Simran Kalita

(Translated)
Now what

Now you know how much I loved you
Even when you didn't give me a single drop in return
And admit it
No one could love you more than I did
But go ahead, test it
That if I loved you this much
Then what could I do for the one who comes and gives me
that love in return
It's a matter of regret
If you had asked me for everything
I would have gladly given it to you
But you failed to recognize this
And your every demand fell short
So now you know that only I could have loved you this
much
But there's someone out there who will love me more than
anyone ever has
Just like I deserve
And if I loved you this much
Just imagine how much I'll love him
Go ahead, test it.

Afsos ki baat

Pyaar toh main usse aaj bhi utni hi karti hoon
Lekin iss pyaar ke upar aur khud ke upar haq sirf mera hai
Woh mujhse koi nahi cheen sakta hai

Mera pyaar itna halka nahi hai ki yeh sab hone ke baad ek
baarish se samundar mein doob jaayega
Kyunki maine sacche dil se tumhe chaha
Aur ab jab chaha, toh nahi chahne ke baawajood bhi tumse
pyaar karti rahungi
Jab tak dil ko poori tasalli milti hai

Tumse pyaar karne ke liye tum ho ya na ho
Koi farq nahi padta
Khush raho, kisi aur ko woh pyaar do
Jo main tumhe nahi de paayi

Hazaar baar apne aap se poochti rahi
Kyun maine tumse pyaar kiya
Kyun maine tumhare hi liye mannat maangti rahi
Phir jaake ehsaas hua
Ki tumse pyaar karna mere taqdeer mein likha hua tha,
aasmaan mein qaid hona likha hua tha

Ab tumse na pyaar karna shayad mere bas ki baat nahi hai
Kaise bhool paaungi
Tumhare khwaab ne mujhe khwaab dekhna sikhaya tha
Afsos iss baat ki nahi hai
Tumko kis mooh se kahoon, kin aankhon se jhaankhoon

(Translated)
A matter of regret

I still love him just as much today
But this love, and the right over myself, are mine alone
No one can take that away from me

My love is not so shallow that after all this a single rainfall
can drown it in the ocean
Because I loved you with all my heart
And now that I've loved you, even if I don't want to
anymore, I'll keep loving you
Until this heart finds fulfillment

Loving you doesn't depend
On whether you're here or not
It makes no difference
Be happy, give that love to someone else
The love I couldn't give to you

A thousand times I tried reasoning with myself
Why did I love you
Why did I keep wishing for you
Then I finally realized
That loving you was written in my destiny, being
imprisoned under the skies was already written

Perhaps not loving you anymore is beyond me
How could I ever forget
Your dreams taught me how to dream
This is not a matter of regret
With what words, what eyes do I look at you

Khud ko gaddaar bana bithaaya hai
Khud se roothi hui hoon
Itna pyaar
Kis liye?
Jawaab khud ko pata nahi, tumko kya bataoon

Tumse kuch nahi chahiye
Maine tumse pyaar kiya
Toh main hi nibhaaoon
Apna kal khud hi likhoon
Aur iss wajah se yeh bhi jaanti hoon ki tumse yeh pyaar
karna ek din zaroor chhod doongi

Likha hua hai
Main rahoon ya na rahoon
Tum acche bane rehna
Kyunki agar woh nahi raha, toh mera pyaar bhi bekaar
chala jaayega
Mujhe yeh dikha do ki main pyaar karne mein sahi thi

Nahi toh main toot jaaungi
Uss sach ko lekar
Ki tum woh kabhi nahi the jo maine tumko socha
Kabhi kaabil nahi the
Tabhi shayad apne aap ko maaf kar paungi

Mere pyaar ko haarne mat do
Mujhko kabhi mat apnaana par meri duaaon ko zaroor
apnaana
Nahi toh bhagwan ko bheji chitthi pahunchne se pehle jala
di jaayegi
Mere pyaar, meri umeed ko kabhi mat thukraana

I've become a traitor to myself
Angry with my own self
So much love
For what?
I don't have the answer myself, what do I tell you

I don't want anything from you
I have loved you
So I must fulfill it myself
I need to write my own tomorrow
And because of this I also know that one day I will surely
quit loving you

It has been written
Whether I stay or not
You must remain good
Because if that doesn't sustain, then my love will have been
wasted
Show me, prove to me, that I was right to love you

Else I will shatter
Carrying the truth
That you were never the person I thought you were
That you were never worthy
Only then I will be able to forgive myself

Don't let my love be defeated
Don't ever make me yours but please accept my prayers
Otherwise the letter I sent to God will be burned before it
ever reaches
Don't reject my love, that hope

Aur tumhari nayi dulhan ko waise sajaana
Jaise chaand aur sitaare hamaare aasmaan ko sajaate hain
Usse hamesha khush rakhna
Kabhi uski aankhon mein aansoon aane mat dena

Aisa nahi hai ki main apne aap ko kurbaan kar rahi hoon
Par bohot bhaag liya
Khud se, tumse, sachai se
Apni hi behrehmi se
Ab thak gayi hoon

Afsos ki baat hogi agar sab kuch aasaani se mit jaaye
Par tumse pyaar karne ki himmat se
Mere khud ke prem ki katha, jab ek din hogi
Toh kitni shaandaar hogi
Jab mera saajan aayega
Uss din tum mere liye naachna
Jaise main aaj tumhare liye naach rahi hoon

Tumse pyaar na karna mujhe mat kehna
Tumse pyaar karke hi apne aap ko paaya hai
Aur apna pyaar ek din zaroor milega
Agar tum nahi toh woh jiske saath mera janmon ka rishta
bana hua hai
Shiddat se pyaar kiya hai toh shiddat se pyaar milega
Iss baat ka mujhe koi afsos nahi.

And decorate your new bride
The way the moon and stars decorate our sky
Always keep her happy
Never let tears enter her eyes

It's not that I am sacrificing myself
But I ran a lot
From myself, from you, from the truth
From my own cruelty
Now I am tired

It will be a matter of regret if everything fades away easily
But with the courage to love you
One day the story of my own love will be written
And it will be so magnificent
When my beloved arrives
Dance for me that day
Just as I am dancing for you today

Don't ask me not to love you
Loving you has helped me find myself
And one day my love will find its destination
If not you then the one with whom my bond of lifetimes is
written with
If you love deeply, then you will be loved deeply
There are no regrets to this matter.

About the author

Simran Kalita is a poetess, actor, singer-songwriter, and filmmaker. She was born in India and grew up in the United States. She attended college at Northeastern University where she received a degree in Computer Science and has attended the Lee Strasberg Theatre & Film Institute and American Academy of Dramatic Arts in New York. She began writing poems at the age of 10 and started a private blog at age 16. The poems in this book span the years between the beginning of that blog to a few months after she graduated college.

www.ingramcontent.com/pod-product-compliance
Lightning Source LLC
Chambersburg PA
CBHW062155120626
46550CB00012B/1555